Signs of Childness in Children's Books

PETER HOLLINDALE

The right word
is always a power,
and communicates its
definiteness to our action.

George Eliot, *Middlemarch*
(Chapter 21, Bk 3)

THIMBLE PRESS

Signs of Childness in Children's Books
comes from The Thimble Press,
publishers since January 1970 of the thrice-yearly journal
Signal Approaches to Children's Books
and other writings on literature and literacy.

First published 1997 by
THE THIMBLE PRESS
Lockwood, Station Road, Woodchester
Stroud, Glos. GL5 5EQ
0145387 3716 phone   0145387 8599 fax

British Library Cataloguing-in-Publication Data
A catalogue record for this book is available from the
British Library

Printed in Great Britain
by Short Run Press, Exeter

ISBN 0 903355 44 2

SIGNS OF CHILDNESS IN CHILDREN'S BOOKS

CONTENTS

I

The Uniqueness of
Children's Literature

Father: Stop behaving like a child!
Son: But I *am* a child!
    (*Hook*, a film by Steven Spielberg)

This short book is an exercise in definition. Although the study of children's literature has expanded in range and developed in sophistication over the last few decades, no one working in the field can be sure that we—those of us who write, teach, review or study children's books—possess a shared and unconfused vocabulary to embody our shared concerns. The concept of 'children's literature' itself is open to several definitions, and potentially useful discussions and debates can go awry as a result of undeclared disagreements about the meanings attached to basic terms of reference. This problem is by no means unique to children's literature, but particular difficulties impinge upon the world of children's books because of the nature of the literature and its readership. A brief study of this kind cannot hope to resolve them. I hope, more modestly, to clarify them.

The exchange between Peter Banning and his son Jack in Steven Spielberg's *Hook* encapsulates our trouble. A host of possible assumptions and attitudes lies behind the simple words. When Peter Banning says 'Stop behaving like a child!', he is *constructing* childhood as a typical set of immature and undesirable behaviours which responsible young persons should abandon. The actual age of the boy he is talking to is disconnected in his mind from the conventional, or theorized age which he associates with his son's behaviour. A 'child' in his reproof is not a living boy but a cliché for irresponsible conduct.

Adult auto-speak of disapproval has obscured his awareness of other meanings the word 'child' might have, not to mention the fact that he is talking to one. Jack's bright response is therefore devastating. He is indeed a child, by biological definition, and therefore presumably entitled to behave, not like one, but as one. His use of the word implies not only his stage of biological development but his entitlement to appropriate behaviour. Jack's father, quite literally, does not know what he is talking about.

Often, when we talk about children's literature, we do not know what we are talking about either. The problem lies above all in the two words of the term itself. Almost without noticing it, in using the term we find ourselves prioritizing either the children or the literature, so that half the term slides into cliché and inertia. Because it would be foolish to ignore either the book or the intended reader in our discussion of children's literature, and because our purposes are many and we cannot always be even-handedly recognizing both, we need a spectrum or sliding scale of working definitions, and to avoid confusion we owe it to our readers to explain which one we are using.

Even if we do prioritize one word or the other, the child or the book, and say so, the prospects for confusion remain substantial. What do we mean by 'children'? And what do we mean by 'literature'? And when we join the two words, have we excluded certain possibilities which might otherwise attach to each? If children's literature is owned by children, as the term implies, is it by inference owned only by those children who can read it (and are therefore sufficiently competent readers) or who are interested in reading it (and are therefore sufficiently willing readers) or who can cope with its emotional demands without being bored or irritated by its constraints of emotional scope (and are therefore developmentally appropriate readers)? Does the term, in fact, circumscribe the available meanings of 'children'? And if the literature is owned by children, is it therefore not owned by adults? In meeting the needs of an immature audience, does it inevitably omit the necessary interests of a mature one? In order to read it, must we disrobe ourselves of our maturity, at least in part, in order to read as a child reads? Are we unavoidably stepping back, whether in nostalgia or condescension or escape, in order to reoccupy a prior self? Is it indeed possible to do this? Or are we simply selecting those elements of our maturity which we share with children, and merging the unchanging continuities of our humanness, while putting aside those parts of ourselves which came later? After all, we cannot ever be comprehensively ourselves; there is never a moment when the whole of our being is in action. So there is nothing more inherently retrogressive in reading a children's book than there is in playing tennis or doing our tax return. Alternatively, are we adults, in reading children's literature, reading the same text but a different book?

In asking questions such as these, whether about children or literature, we are concerning ourselves with reading and with readers, with definitions that attend to suitability, preference and response. It is quite possible for books to be enthusiastically read by people for whom they were not 'intended', in this case adults, yet still not qualify for entry to the literature that these same adults might be expected to choose. When we define a literature by its readership, and signal that readership as by definition immature, are we saying that whatever incidental pleasure it may give to mature adults there is still an absolute standard for the word 'literature' which makes the qualification 'children's' tacitly reductive? Is children's literature not really literature at all? Is it a mere courtesy title, like the earldoms given to the eldest sons of English dukes while they wait for their fathers to die, giving intermediate status but no power? Or like the degree of Bachelor of Arts in ancient universities, when it was awarded to boy graduates until they grew up and became Masters of Arts instead? Children's literature may by implication be provisional and intermediate literature, called so by grudging courtesy (as Henry James intended when he wrote of the 'literature, as it may be called for convenience, of children') but not real literature at all.

A parallel worth testing may be found with the growth of the women's movement and of 'women's studies', as a branch of academe. There now exists a literature of fictions written, or deemed to be written, essentially by women for women. The possibility of true readings of these fictions, it is argued, is determined by the politics of gender. There is nothing to stop a man from reading these key feminist texts, but the male reader is biologically disenfranchised from reading them as women readers can, and the incapacity cannot be erased no matter how sympathetic he may be to the women's cause. A male reader cannot read a novel by, say, Margaret Atwood as a woman reads it, just as an adult cannot read a novel by, say, Roald Dahl as a child reads it.

A politics of gender determines the status of women's fiction, and whether or not a valid analogy can be drawn with children's literature depends in turn on a politics of childhood. Some differences are obvious. Women are biologically mature, just as men are, so the differences are lateral and permanent, not developmental and temporary. There are few areas of psychological and emotional experience which are closed to women in terms of direct experience, and none at all in terms of knowledge and awareness, but considerably more which are closed to children before puberty, or should be. Women writers are writing for women readers with whom they can have reciprocal articulate conversation, meeting as nonconcessionary equals. Writers for children can rarely have conversations of this kind with their readers without filtering their adulthood through a protective gauze, however thin, and making allowance for children's social, emotional and linguistic inexperience.

The analogy has manifest limitations, but just how severe these limitations are depends on our degree of willingness to accord childhood a status, a value, an experiential uniqueness, in its own right. If we see childhood only as a prelude, as a provisional phase marked by gradually fading limitations, then the analogy only implies that literature does not have to be universal in order to be significant, but can be addressed to specific and exclusive audiences. If on the other hand we see childhood as a Prelude, in Wordsworth's sense, containing unique experiences accessible to adults only as knowledge and memory, then the literature *as read by children* may be marked by indigenous distinctive qualities as well as limitations. Either way, to write books for children, and to write about them, is a political act.

The crucial limitation of the analogy is, however, self-evident. The women's movement writes its own books, and children do not. The transaction between woman writer and woman reader is one of equals, engaged in simultaneous experience both within and outside the text. That is to say, although there may be a historical and cultural gap dividing author from reader, it can be minimal. There can be a virtual mutuality of language and experience. The novel's address and reception may be almost epistolary in nature, and the implied reader possesses latent reciprocal fictions which might immediately be written in response.

The writer for children and the child reader are differently placed. Only in very informal ways do children write stories for other children, and publication, if it happens at all, is usually local—school magazines, wall displays, or in scurrilous instances a furtive passing round under the desks. The dignity of print and access to an unknown, conjectural audience is a rare event. It does happen—some distinguished examples include *The Far-Distant Oxus* by Katharine Hull and Pamela Whitlock, *Sabre, the Horse from the Sea* by Kathleen Herald (K.M. Peyton), and *The Outsiders* by S.E. Hinton—but such books are usually written, as these were, by teenagers in that stage of life which is neither child nor adult but which I shall wish to emphasize as youth. Poems and stories by younger children do appear—prize-winning entries in national competitions, or work inspired by exceptional teachers—but the total is not great.

Aside from such exceptional instances, it would still be wrong to say there is no literature by children for children. What there is consists of jokes, scatological updatings of familiar songs and rhymes, subversive parodies and satires, an oral culture largely directed at mockery of the adult status quo: the flourishing literary underclass of the school playground which was so meticulously documented by Iona and Peter Opie. The

Internet is now a possible global playground, with consequences it is still too soon to see.

A conventional printed literature by children for children, however, does not exist. It is produced for them by adults. Unlike the 'woman's novel' written by a woman (or the 'man's novel' written by a man), the children's book cannot normally be a culturally simultaneous transaction between author and reader. It is written, in part, from memory, because the author's childhood is over. The author must construct childhood from an amalgam of personal retrospect, acquaintance with contemporary children, and an acquired system of beliefs as to what children are, and should be, like. Between the author and the child there is a cultural and historical gap, almost always of at least half a generation, usually much more. The conversation of minds between author and reader (relayed through its intermediate messengers such as narrator and protagonist) is different in nature from the conversation of the adult novel—and, significantly, different in nature from the conversation which takes place when the children's book is read by an adult. In this, it seems to me, children's literature is unique, and different in kind from other forms of literature. And the implications of the difference are far-reaching. The author's textual negotiations with the child about the meaning and nature of childhood are a distinguishing feature of children's books, and an intrinsic part of the critic's terms of reference.

We do not have a word to represent the content of these fictive negotiations about childhood. In the following pages I shall propose one, and examine where the use of it might lead.

Exactly how this cultural time-gap matters depends again on our politics of childhood and our sense of the status of children. If we see childhood as essentially preparatory and developmental, a long and gradual rehearsal for maturity (marked probably by a stormy dress rehearsal in mid-adolescence), then we shall emphasize the processes of learning and growing and acquiring which the early years entail: a child will always for us be in transit, on the way to being something more developed

12

and advanced (our adult selves). Seeing the child herself as provisional, we shall be inclined to notice the provisional and elementary qualities of what she reads. Therefore, we shall value children's books for their educative qualities, even if we take a humane and generous view of what education is—even if we value education of the emotions and imagination as highly as we value intellectual and linguistic development or the acquisition of knowledge.

If on the other hand we see childhood as an autonomous part of life, and its passage as entailing some losses as well as many gains, if we see it as a phase of experience which cannot be curtailed or repressed without lasting harm to the adult, we shall place less store by the developmental usefulness of children's activities and more by the help they give in enabling the child to be a child. The fragment of conversation between Peter and Jack Banning neatly polarizes these two points of view. Valuing childhood for its own sake, we are likely to be more alert to its varying nature, its fits and starts, advances and retreats, its day-to-day capriciousness. We are more likely both to expect a lot and put up with a lot. We are more likely to grin and bear the muddle and inconsistency of children's reading, and not find it particularly strange if a ten-year-old is reading *Jane Eyre* one day and Enid Blyton the next.

The two positions are artificially polarized in this account. However much we value childhood, we see it as a process of development. All children, except one, grow up, and who would wish to be the parent or teacher of the one? And there are not many Gradgrinds around these days, requiring a Dickens to remind them that childhood exists. All the same, differences of emphasis are widespread in modern adult society. It is a historical commonplace that the question 'What is a child?' would be answered differently in different historical periods. Modern historians, led by the pioneering work of Philippe Ariès, have drawn attention to the historicity of childhood as a concept. Although the differences may be more subtle, we must also be alert to different understandings of childhood among contemporaries, even among adults who belong to the same culture and work professionally with or on behalf of children. Where the balance falls for us as individuals in the polarized views described above will strongly affect the way we evaluate children's books, and still more importantly the way we write about and read them. The adjustment of vocabulary suggested in this book is designed to clarify such differences.

In particular, the weight we attach to developmentalism in children's experience will decide what importance we give to children's own consciousness of childhood. All children know for a period of years that they are indeed children, and hold culturally determined views of what childhood is, what its privileges and drawbacks are, and how long it lasts. They all have yardsticks by which to measure childhood, acquired unconsciously and effortlessly from parents, other adults, schools, peer-groups, and recreational media of various kinds. The sense of what is appropriate and what is permitted to children is socially acquired, from other children and from adults of varying attitudes and competence. Is that all that is necessary? Do we see childhood self-awareness as a naturally occurring, socially conditioned phenomenon determined by immediate environment, one which it is important for responsible adults to guide and influence in a process of continuous adjustment as the child grows up? Or is it a question also of imagination? Is your life as a child affected by what you imagine a child to be? Is the business of being a child in truth a creative one, not merely a responsive one? I have suggested already that adult writers construct childhood when they write for and about children, and in the wake of modern literary studies this is uncontentious. It is a small step from that to suggesting that children also construct childhood as they go along, and that they do so from fictions of various kinds, not merely from social experience.

Two inferences follow, one obvious and uncontroversial, the other open to challenge. The first is that children are affected by the images of childhood they encounter, whether in real life or in various forms of story, and that certain images can be damaging, by causing emotional distress or inciting antisocial behaviour. The second is that, if childhood is indeed an imaginative

14

construct for the child, children need to come across a vari-
egated imaginary world of childhood, a multiplicity of childhood possibilities, which will enrich and diversify their sense of
what it can mean to be a child, both in itself and as a stage en
route to being something else. They need, that is, to meet children outside their actual lives. This is close to saying that in the
modern world there is a need for children's fictions about children, and that a necessary phase of growth will be impoverished
if these are missing. However, if we do say that children need
imaginary children, does it follow that they need to find them
in books?

Even those critics most anxious to promote children's reading
would not necessarily place great emphasis on reading about
children. Perhaps this is especially true of those who value the
developmental role of books and reading. Brian Alderson, in his
influential essay 'The Irrelevance of Children to the Children's
Book Reviewer', attacked the practice of lazy reviewers in citing the opinions of ready-to-hand children as evidence of quality in children's books. He wrote:

> Critics who abdicate their responsibilities like this probably forget
> a number of things that are of considerable importance if the adult
> is to be of any help in creating intelligently literate young people.
> In calling upon the views of children he may forget that he is
> almost bound to receive opinions that are immature and often
> inarticulate . . . once one assigns to reading the vital role, which I
> believe it has, of making children more perceptive and more aware
> of the possibilities of language, then it becomes necessary to hold
> fast to qualitative judgements formed upon the basis of adult ex-
> perience. Naturally a knowledge of and sympathy with children
> (beyond mere remembrance of things past) must play a vital part in
> this judgement . . .

Alderson's essay is a classic statement of the objective, professional view of children's literature and reading, at its most
cogent and austere. He is impatient with the slackness of

impressionistic subjectivity, whether it is obtained from convenient stand-by children or quarried from personal memories.
His view of the reviewer's task is to provide a qualitative literary
judgement based on resources of experienced professional reading.

This disciplined approach must surely form part of effective
critical practice on children's literature. But what is noticeable
here is the association between professional judgements and a
developmental view of literature's role in children's lives. The
object is to create 'intelligently literate young people', to make
children 'more perceptive and more aware of the possibilities of
language'. These are excellent aims, but their implied emphasis
is on the adult-in-the-making rather than the child now, the
process rather than the state, potential rather than current experience. By pushing childhood, actual or remembered, to the
unprofessional margins, Alderson makes his priorities still
clearer.

So while this must be part of good practice, it cannot in my
view be all of it, because it undervalues the presentness of childhood, and hence the instabilities of maturity and taste that char-
acterize children's reading. It is, so to speak, a statement about
children's *literature* rather than *children's* literature. And its particular incompleteness (not error) lies in omitting the possibility
that a necessary part of the child's imaginative spectrum of
childhood might only be provided in those children's books
that professional critics are likely to deride. To satisfy some of
the essential needs of childhood, the child's subjective, inarticu-
late taste and the adult's sentimental memory may give a subversive, accurate, complementary signal to set beside the literary
judgement.

Where in all this possible reading, one must ask, do we find the
childhood and the children who can help the reader to construct her childhood of imagination? Where and of what kind is
the childhood in the books?

This part of children's literature's terms of reference may not
matter if children come across imaginary childhoods some-

where else—in films, on television and video. Provided that imaginary childhood reaches beyond the child's own life, there may be no particular reason why it should do so through the printed word.

In practice, however, it seems that the media cannot be trusted to supply imaginary childhoods. On the contrary, they may well be partly to blame for the marked foreshortening of childhood that is evident in modern western societies. As Ariès and others have shown, the duration of childhood is historically variable. Perhaps we have simply entered a period when it is short. This may cause problems when in other respects (length of compulsory school attendance, delay in starting work, a vacuum of social and economic usefulness) childhood is simultaneously very long. While they are still children, protractedly in certain ways, boys and girls watch television films and soap operas and other popular dramatic fictions which are almost exclusively about grown-ups and teenagers with grown-up concerns. The child whose fantasy life is built from these programmes is obliged to construct an imaginative childhood out of fictions of adult behaviour, not children's. Even without passing judgement on the sorts of adult behaviour to be witnessed in these programmes, it is hardly surprising if some disturbing behavioural developments ensue.

There are of course television plays and series about children, shown at the time of day allotted for children's viewing. In Britain the pioneering example of such drama is *Grange Hill*, a classroom soap opera about the life of a comprehensive school. This is a very popular programme, and for thousands of children it has probably supplied the most important point where the childhood of experience and the childhood of imagination meet. *Grange Hill* presents dramatic versions of the typical, or is perceived to do so by its viewers. Therefore the programme itself and reactions to it have a lot to tell us about modern childhood. The way the series constructs childhood, and relations between child and adult, externalizes a set of beliefs on the part of writers and producers about what is true, what is real, and what is acceptable in current child behaviour, especially at school. It embodies a kind of observant documentary imagining of childhood on the part of adults, enlivened by the artifice of heightened and concentrated incident, the exaggeration of immediacy, which distinguishes most drama from the uneventful routines of everyday life. And it also embodies implicit judgements on what is desirable in child behaviour, how children and adults manage their relationships and how they ought to do so, and where (if anywhere) the boundary line of permissible conduct is drawn.

When children watch *Grange Hill*, and later quasi-documentary fictions about youth, they bring their own construction of childhood to bear on their response: they find some people and incidents convincing and some not, they distribute approval and condemnation, admiration and scorn, identification and rejection, according to their existing self-awareness, which may in turn be modified by their experience of the programme. And the judgements children make may agree with those the programme's writers anticipate, or differ from them. This transaction is multiple: no two children are likely to respond in exactly the same way, and there are certain to be differing reactions among children of differing social, ethnic, cultural and regional groups. Children at a London comprehensive will react differently from those at a prep school in Cornwall. Children at two London comprehensives are also likely to react differently, perhaps more subtly but also perhaps more importantly, depending on the similarities they recognize between their own schools and neighbourhoods and those they see depicted.

If there were many programmes of this kind, so that children came across a range of fictional school childhoods in their television viewing, no one programme would be especially significant. But there are not. Series such as this are expensive to make, represent a long-term investment, and anyway are competing for time in only a few hours of designated children's television, most of which can be filled with cheaper products. So any series such as *Grange Hill* (whatever its country of origin) is culturally a very important phenomenon, representing one of relatively few media sources where the child can test her childhood against a childhood of imagination. Commercial production and competition for audiences can generate a standardized construction of childhood and youth which interacts significantly with the constructed childhood of its viewers.

Fictions of everyday reality are not the only television dramas where children meet children. There are frequent television adaptations of classic or famous children's stories: over the years they have included dramatizations of modern stories such as *The Owl Service, Tom's Midnight Garden*, and *The Lion, the Witch and the Wardrobe*, as well as established classics such as *Tom Sawyer, The Secret Garden* and *The Box of Delights*. For various reasons, including the financial outlay and competition for time with other kinds of programme, such series are never very plentiful. At best there will only be an hour or two a week when children have access to programmes of this kind. But suppose that there were more of these productions. Suppose it was decided as a matter of policy that our 'literary heritage' of fiction about childhood should be mediated through the screen because for many children the book cannot compete with it. Would anything be seriously lost?

It goes without saying that initiatives of this sort would not help Brian Alderson's purpose of creating 'intelligently literate young people'. The developmental cause of awakening imagination through discoveries of language would not profit and might well be harmed. And since this general objective must cover at least half the professional goals of those concerned with children's literature, there would not be much to cheer about. But the other half of what I am suggesting here, the need for children to construct their childhoods of the mind through their encounters with imagined ones, might well be helped by such extensions of what is available outside the printed word.

Almost anything (short of what would cause emotional or behavioural damage) is better than nothing, but there are practical considerations as well as principles which dictate that the screen can be no substitute for the book.

One obvious practical difficulty is that children in television drama can only be played by children. Just as children's literature, with marginal exceptions, cannot be written by children, so here again we meet the intrinsic limitations of childhood. The problem is not nearly so intractable as with writing. Many children are natural and accomplished actors, and by no means only those who go to stage schools. Some excellent performances have been given by children, and the standard is remarkably high. Even so, a uniform, sustained high quality of child acting is very difficult to achieve, and simply cannot routinely match the practised competence of adult players. Although children can do many things well, there is unavoidably a limitation of emotional range and understanding on the part of young actors. With rare exceptions, it is a fact (and not, perhaps, altogether regrettable) that children cannot convincingly act many of the things that children regularly do, experience and feel. Children's literature is full of episodes which it would not be fair to ask a child to play.

In any event, there are elements of what is best and most valuable in children's literature which it is difficult, even impossible, to dramatize. The adventures of children on their own, in sequences of action where there is little dialogue, can only be filmed at best as external events—occurrences which on film can represent the outward plight of a child but not her inner state. But it is precisely the conjunction of exterior with interior action, and the suspense of exciting situations made more real and vivid because we share the unspoken thoughts and feelings of the child protagonist, which give the children's book its special place in helping a reader to build and diversify her sense of childhood possibility. This expansion through imagined action of the inward self is something that the book can do and films, on the whole, cannot. In reading, children can share an imagined child's solitude in a way that other media do not permit.

For all these reasons, ranging from constraints of programming to inherent limitations of the visual media, the representation of childhood for children on the film and television screen is sparse and incomplete, and in danger moreover of giving undue prominence to a few influential models. Otherwise, children who do not read books are exposed to a fictional life made up almost exclusively of adults. What we see is—to use an ugly word for a fairly ugly phenomenon—the defictionalizing of childhood. Except in the children's book, most fictions that children meet omit the child, unless as fantasized proto-adult, and especially they omit the child's interior life expressed through action. The media have turned fictional children into an endangered species, and children's literature is their conservation area.

There is, in my view, no substitute for the book, and for the child in the book. To return, then, to the distinctive nature of children's literature. Many differences have been proposed between children's literature and literature for adults, and many pragmatic definitions suggested. Most of these have had one or both of two effects. First, they have drawn a dividing line between the two literatures, mirroring the obvious differences between the two stages of human life. Second, because they see childhood as a preparatory and developmental phase (which everyone agrees that it is) but not always as a life experience with its own intrinsic value and uniqueness (which not everyone agrees that it is), they have customarily downgraded the literature accordingly, viewing it as a simple and provisional experiment with complexities to come. I shall be reviewing some of these definitions and assumptions in the next chapter. The conventional reply to such reductive judgements is the assertion that 'a good book for children is a good book for anybody', which is a splendid principle but begs a lot of questions. Not least, it skirts around the question whether the child and the adult read the same text when they read the same words.

What is truly unusual, however, is the relation between the author and the reader. This difference is not unique to the book and the printed word, as I have tried to show in discussing *Grange Hill*. It is shared by all adult artistic and imaginative performances for children, and is as true of visual images and picture books as it is of words. The distinctive feature is that all such artwork is in part a one-way traffic. Children, by the nature of their stage in life, cannot respond with full articulacy to the works they read and watch. When children's reviews of children's books are published, as they sometimes are, the limitations are easy to see. Still less can children respond with reciprocal artworks of their own, *at equivalent levels of technical competence and maturity.* This is true even of the most seemingly 'childish' of works for children. Children can respond with artworks, which have experiential value and considerable interest and merit. Their reactions to stories, through narrative continuations or paintings, are often witty, astute and insightful, often artistically shaped. But they are not fully reciprocal in the way that is latently possible for adult readers of adult authors. There is a gap of time, of maturity, along with separation generated by an ever-fluctuating culture, which cuts off adult author from child reader. To put the matter brutally, the adult children's author is always obsolete. He or she can never inhabit the *presentness* of childhood.

So the childhood established by the author in a text for children is a construct, made from various resources which can compensate for dispossession.

The lack of scope for artistic and verbal reciprocity, however, is only part of the story. The other part is suggested by those varied children in their varied cultural circumstances who watch *Grange Hill.* The child too has a pre-existent construct of childhood, and the responsive and judgemental power which comes from occupying the presentness of childhood, in her own time and place. The critic of children's literature needs a language to explore the transaction that occurs when these two constructs meet. Taking a series of particular perspectives, I shall attempt to define the adult side of this transaction.

2

Meanings and Valuations of Children's Literature

Empirical definitions of children's literature are legion, and some of them now famous. In this section I shall consider a few of the existing formulations, in order to argue that the only secure grounds for definition are those that rest in the exchange between adult author and child reader of complex constructions of childhood. For this process of construction we need a defining term, which I shall present in the next chapter. For the moment, the key word in this introduction is 'exchange'. There is a further literature which expresses complex constructions of childhood, but without anticipating that children will participate as readers in its utterance. This is the literature, now extensive, which consists of fictions about childhood for the adult. Undeniably there is a literature for adults about children which is rarely if ever accessible to a child. However, the reverse is not true. All children's literature is accessible to adults. Some of it is interesting only to immature adults or to those who read professionally on behalf of children. But a great deal of it has readings to offer to the adult which are very different from children's readings and valuable in their own right. Much critical wariness, controversy and self-protection circle around this last point.

In the following discussion, then, I shall start with broad areas of definition and go on to more detailed questions of authorial attitudes and adult reader response.

In his book *The Compass of Irony* D.C. Muecke says this:

> ... even without bringing into consideration the fact that the concept of irony is still evolving, we can see that the diversity of the

forms of irony multiplied by the diversity of approaches to irony ... and the difficulty of distinguishing it ... might themselves explain why there has not been any adequate classification of irony ... no brief and simple definition that will include all kinds of irony while excluding all that is not irony.

If we substitute 'children's literature' for 'irony' throughout this passage we find our predicament exactly summarized, and incidentally observe to our comfort that we are not alone in our terminological uncertainties.

The most comprehensive definition I know is advanced by Peter Hunt in his study *Criticism, Theory and Children's Literature*, and having floated it he promptly recognizes that it is unmanageably wide:

> We define children's literature, then, according to our purposes—which, after all, is what all definitions do: they divide the world according to our needs. Children's literature, disturbingly enough, can quite reasonably be defined as books read by, especially suitable for, or especially satisfying for, members of the group currently defined as children. However, such an accommodating definition is not very practical, as it obviously includes every text ever read by a child, so defined.

In seeking to fence in this agoraphobic definition, Hunt asserts the ephemerality of children's literature, affected as it is by swift changes in historical concepts of childhood, and proposes a narrower definition while carefully insisting that it is only partial:

> On the whole, then, that a particular text was written expressly for children who are recognizably children, with a childhood recognizable today, must be part of the definition ...

The problem with this formulation is that, while it duly takes account of both the author and the reader, it omits the generic text. To write 'expressly for children', as we shall see, can mean

24

many things, and is certainly not restricted to consciously and deliberately implying a present-day child as your reader, so in this definition authorial interest in child readers, which is a wide and relevant phenomenon, is narrowed to authorial intention of writing for children, which excludes much writing that children commonly accept. Another problem is that no book can 'expressly' be written for unknown yet 'recognized' children of the future, so that only contemporary work for contemporary readers could ever qualify.

On the other side of the exchange, to confine the genre to ephemeral constitutions of its readership is to impose unreal precision upon an increasingly unstable concept. Children take their time about ceasing to be children, going through long periods of being children when they feel like it and not when they don't, and the adult world finds it on the whole convenient to accept the fact. A partial definition such as Hunt's calls for something akin to the precise boundaries which are observed in (for example) certain African societies, where a single initiation rite marks the passage from child to adult. Later I shall be considering a symbolic rite of passage, and what it tells us about useful meanings and extensions of 'children's literature'. Such rites may centre upon isolated significant events, as I shall show, but they occur across a span of years which forbids us to locate transitions at specific, culturally determined ages. An important feature of modern western societies is that our communal and official recognitions of childhood's end are arbitrary, inconsistent and ritualistically barren. We live in an age of do-it-yourself repudiations of childhood. Lacking dependable and socially esteemed waymarks (equivalents of the first wage packet), children and teenagers often put home-made anti-social waymarks in their place (joyriding, for example). If things go wrong, childhood may then be pleaded in mitigation of precociously adult misdemeanours. Socially we pay the penalty for giving children hopelessly mixed signals, and in children's literature we see evidence of our confusion.

In the following discussion, then, I shall be seeking to locate children's literature not just in such external factors but in features of the text. The effect will be to suggest more specific and limited distinctions between children's and adults' literature than many previous discussions have assumed.

If we look at several statements by children's authors on their primary concerns (and the following well-known ones are representative of many) we find that they are first of all interested in *what* they are writing and only as an afterthought in who it is for. One of the most famous is Arthur Ransome's:

True?

> You write not *for* children but for yourself, and if, by good fortune, children enjoy what you enjoy, why then you are a writer of children's books.

John Rowe Townsend, writing in *The Horn Book*, said much the same thing :

> ...if the books that come naturally to a writer happen to be highly popular with children, so much the better for him and so much the better for them. But he is not obliged to appeal to every child ... His job is to write the best book he can.

And so did C.S. Lewis, in his essay 'On Three Ways of Writing for Children', describing the third way 'which is the only one I could ever use myself: [it] consists in writing a children's story because a children's story is the best art-form for something you have to say ...'

There are other possible attitudes, such as the one characterized by Lewis as 'giving them what they want'. And of course authorial protestations must be taken with a pinch of salt. But so commonplace are statements of this sort, one cannot help concluding that the existence of children is a happy accident for children's writers, because it gives them an excuse for doing what they want to do. After all, the other side of the transaction cannot be forgotten. The 'children's story' is only the 'best art-form' because children will like to read it; otherwise the art-form may be the same but the name for it will not. If children do 'enjoy what you do', it is because you have invested something in the text which causes them to. That is to say, the fact of a child readership is testament to the existence in the book of properties which the author, often for non-commercial reasons, desired to put there. And when the purpose *is* commercial, even if cynically so, a book or story will not succeed unless its construction of childhood satisfies a sufficient number of children.

In view of these compendious definitions, and the failure of attempts at inclusiveness in categorizing either author or reader, we can sympathize with the sensible pragmatic defeatism of John Rowe Townsend when he wrote: 'The only practical definition of a children's book today—absurd as it sounds—is "a book which appears on the children's list of a publisher".' I shall therefore place it first in the following list of broad definitions, which are set out not in order of merit but proceeding from production to available readership to historical readership to genre to texts to reading event. Together they seem to me to represent the available agenda of possible categories:

1. Children's literature is a body of work forming the combined outcome of intentions and decisions on the part of authors, publishers and booksellers. It includes a corporate commercial design on the child market.

2. Children's literature is a body of writing collectively so defined because it has proven or likely appeal to present-day children in the prevailing circumstances of childhood.

3. Children's literature is a body of writing collectively so defined because it appeals or has appealed to children in the present or the past.

4. Children's literature is a genus of fictions which is concerned with children, or with imaginary figures or situations widely understood by children as relevant to them, and which is linguistically accessible to children.

5. Children's literature is an aggregation of texts with certain features in common, which enable them to establish meaningful transactions with child readers (and which incidentally may also enable them to do so with adults).

6. Children's literature does not denote a text but a reading event. Whenever a successful voluntary transaction takes place between any text and any one child, that text is for that occasion 'children's literature'. (Conversely, when a successful voluntary transaction occurs between any 'children's book' and any one adult, that text is for that occasion 'literature', not 'children's literature'.)

All of these definitions have merits and usefulness. One thing I wish to argue is that children's literature studies would be greatly helped if critics took care to signify which of them is primarily in use on any given occasion (or which other, since I cannot lay claim to comprehensiveness). Other potentially useful definitions would concern questions of child psychology, reading capability, socialization, and so forth. These are important, but they are complementary to literary criticism rather than part of it, so are omitted from my terms of reference here except where I specifically include them. Of these six definitions, it is (4) and (5) which mainly concern me in this book, but a word needs to be said first about (6).

Logically, the first part of this definition seems to me indisputable. Whatever a child reads with pleasure and understanding is de facto 'children's literature'. But its use in this sense devalues the term by flooding it with eccentric particulars. An advanced, sophisticated child might read with pleasure certain novels about children because they invoke a construction of childhood which is meaningful and relevant to the child's own sense of self: L.P. Hartley's *The Go-Between* might be an example. For that child, Hartley's novel is in my view 'children's literature', within the meanings of (6) and (5). But if the book is not 'children's literature' in the broader senses, and if unlike Hartley's novel it does not contain a major construction of childhood, then I think we are wiser to talk of 'a child's literature'.

This term rests on the idea of a 'personal literature', which all habitual readers have. Consider what you would choose if you were obliged to fit all your available future reading into one small bookcase. It is a fair bet that some of the major literary

28

experiences of your life would be sent to the shredder before you would give up certain children's books you recall with special pleasure, or copies of plays you have acted in, or minor novels which happened to excite you, or (as in my case) a set of ornithological field guides. We all have a personal literature of maverick preferences which in the last resort displaces the official literature of our professional lives. Many children start to build this eccentric collection early, and it can include adult works precociously enjoyed. They are not children's literature, but they are a child's literature.

The other half of definition (6) rests on the supposition that we cannot as adults read as a child reads. However good we are at understanding children and recalling childhood, indeed however 'childish' we are, we are disbarred by time and maturity from authentic re-entry into childhood imaginative responses. Whatever we may be doing, we are not constructing our own childhood. We may be *re*constructing it (see Chapter 4) but that is something different. Consequently we are guests at the table of children's literature, *even if we ourselves have written it.* By definition, we are obsolete.

The definition of children's literature which I propose therefore involves the author, the text and the child, but with qualified meanings in each case. The author is a person with imaginative interests in constructing childhood (usually but not necessarily through creating child characters) and who on purpose or accidentally uses a narrative voice and language that are audible to children. The text of children's literature is one in which this construction is present. The reader is a child who is still in the business of constructing his or her own childhood, and aware of its presentness—aware that it is not yet over. Where these conditions co-exist, the *event* of children's literature takes place.

By its nature, the body of text which forms children's literature is capable of many other readings, and they occur when adults (readers who know that their childhood is not a current event) choose to read it. These adults can read in many ways. Peter Hunt distinguishes four modes of adult reading of children's books:

> — to read the books as if they were peer-texts, which is 'to register the presence of, but "read against", the implied readership'
> — to read on behalf of a child, for personal or professional reasons
> — to read the text with an eye to discussing it with other adults
> — to surrender to the book on its own terms. Hunt observes that this 'is as close as we can get to *reading as a child*, but this is a very long way from reading as an actual child does'.

These are very useful distinctions, and cover between them the vast majority of adult readings. To summarize my own definition still further, I would therefore suggest:

> Children's literature is a body of texts with certain common features of imaginative interest, which is activated as children's literature by a reading event: that of being read by a child. A child is someone who believes on good grounds that his or her condition of childhood is not yet over.

This definition recognizes a doubleness we have to live with, namely that children's literature is characterized both by textual status and by readership, and its uniqueness is evident at the point where they meet.

There are, however, three factors which are not wholly accounted for in this effort at precision. First is the point, already noted, that childhood in modern societies ends gradually, not at fixed points. Second is the belief of many adults, including most of those who write and read children's books, that their childhood is still alive in themselves. Third is the belief of other adults that reading children's books is a childish, lazy and escapist thing to do. Each of these needs some comment.

Whether by social ritual or life's accidental shocks, some

people move from child to adult in one fell swoop. Most do not. There is for most people an intermediate phase, when childhood is felt to be over but full adult maturity has not yet been reached. We have various terms for it, notably 'adolescence', and various terms for the literature appropriate to it, notably 'teenage fiction', and 'novels for young adults'. They refer to the phase of life which used to be called 'youth', and it can last a long time. Because in my view we habitually misconceive it, in particular by linking it to a specific age group, by assuming that it is much the same for both sexes, and by needlessly circumscribing our definitions of its literature, I shall give it special consideration in Chapter 7. This is one of several cases where I hope to blur habitual boundaries as well as define them.

It is commonplace in the post-Romantic western sensibility to value the residual childhood that is carried into adult life. This is why most of us would put some of our childhood books in the personal bookcase, and it is one reason why many adults read children's books. They do so because they want to read about children, and thus refresh the links with their own childhood. This is a very widespread, very deep-rooted desire. It is not a Romantic invention; we can find it for instance in Henry Vaughan's fine seventeenth-century poem, 'The Retreat'. Since the Romantics, however, it has been more deeply integrated in the educated consciousness. The effect is visible in this remark in a recent newspaper article on the novelist Ian McEwan: the italics are mine. 'If he writes passionately about childhood . . . this is because, like *most committed fathers*, he wants to retain the influence of the child in himself; or at least to have it as an antidote to the tyrannies of adulthood.'

We can see why a companion piece to Brian Alderson's essay might be called 'The Irrelevance of Children to the Children's Novelist', and why Ransome, Townsend, Lewis and others write about their craft as they do. Childhood and children interest them, rather than child readers. If this is the dynamo of your imagination, it may be a small matter to make the adjustments of voice, address and style which are needed to win you an audience of child readers. (On the other hand it may be a matter of indifference or disinclination or impossibility, as with L.P. Hartley.) Equally, however, we can see that it may be irrelevant to many adult readers whether a particular text is 'for' children or adults, when what matters is that it is a transaction with childhood.

It cannot be said too strongly, however, that retaining the child in yourself is not the same thing as being a child. Once we are adults, the child in ourselves may not be dead, and we may be able to reconstruct a childhood of the mind and imagination, but childhood itself is over. Its *presentness* is irrecoverable. That is the crucial difference, and it is why—in the terms of my definition set out above—as adults we can read children's literature as a body of literary texts, but we cannot *activate* it by reading the text as a child reads.

In spite of our irreversible adulthood and the manifest complexity of reading—on the part of adult and child alike—there are still people eager to draw sharp boundary lines and castigate the adult who reads children's books. A lastingly instructive specimen of such thinking is the essay 'Escape into Childhood' by Mary Warnock. I shall discuss it in detail because it expresses a widespread view with exceptionally lucid intolerance. Because Warnock is a philosopher and employs a strategy of rational persuasion, it is specially revealing to observe the assumptions, emotions and prejudices which underlie the reasonable voice. Warnock was ruffled because her undergraduate house-guests preferred children's books to other forms of mental entertainment:

> There is no doubt that there is an irritating feyness about the spectacle of an intelligent adult refusing to read the newspaper, refusing to go to lectures on contemporary affairs, refusing even to discuss the rights and wrongs of any political party, but instead curling up, metaphorically thumb-sucking, lost in *The Secret Garden* or *Sara Crewe*. One feels inclined to ask how they *can* be intelligent, if they are so ready to switch their minds off when they are not actually working.

32

This is a very revealing passage, not least in its assumption that mature and educated leisure consists properly in absorbing and debating the ephemera of current affairs. As I write, current affairs are dominated by anxiety about the ills and crimes of children. None of the heavyweight papers I have read, nor the politicians I have listened to as a model Warnock adult, have given me remotely as intelligent an insight into these troubles as does the moving demonstration of *mens sana in corpore sano*, the diagnosis of psychosomatic illness, the celebration of therapeutic play, the castigation of parental neglect, the proof of redemptive power in constructive motivation, which I find in *The Secret Garden*. These are not simple matters, but child readers can register them, and so in more sophisticated ways could Warnock's students.

Such matters pass Warnock by because, for her, simplicity is endemic in children's literature, and escapism is what its adult readers are in search of. Her crusty impatience, evident above, is expressed through a careful appearance of fairness and reason. Certain objections to such irresponsible use of adult intelligence are raised only to be scrupulously set aside. Nostalgia, though regrettable, can be historically informative, which is compensatory; people do like escapism, which is regrettable, but escapist books for children can be morally preferable to those for adults; intelligence and imagination are held by some adults to be like muscles, which will atrophy if unused, but Warnock rejects the analogy. The rational philosopher is playing admirably fair, it seems. 'One must be fair.' Then there comes an equation between the imaginative quality of children's literature and adults', and by sleight of argument imagination becomes somehow identified with 'imaginative attention to natural detail'. How does the children's book fare then? 'Why not Beatrix Potter rather than Blake?'

Perhaps the answer is that essentially for Blake, as for Coleridge, the details of natural phenomena were significant of something other than themselves. One may totally reject Blake's vision of the world, or Coleridge's; but the fact that the natural details drawn or

33

described by them *meant* something more, is what renders them imaginatively enlarging for us. To concentrate on the details is to come within range of a vision, whether the vision is intellectually satisfying or not. Whereas, in the case of children's books—even the best of them—the details are observed for their own sake; simply because they are attractive, not because they are significant. Therefore one's imagination is not exercised. It is pleased, but no more than that.

How recently, one wonders, had Warnock read *The Secret Garden*? As many critics have observed, the garden that Mary finds has affinities with the Garden of Eden. In Chapter 23, when the newly strengthening Colin suggests that they should all sit cross-legged under a tree, he remarks that 'It will be like sitting in a sort of temple', and Ben Weatherstaff, who is 'agen' prayer meetin's', joins in. So does Dickon, whose way with animals brings the crow, the fox, the squirrels and the lamb into the circle, in an idealized image of Edenic harmony between all creatures. Earlier in the book, in Chapter 9, when Mary enters the garden for the first time, she sees in its natural, neglected beauty the vestiges of former care, and details are significant. 'She walked under one of the fairy-like grey arches between the trees and looked up at the sprays and tendrils which formed them.' The grey arches are those of a secular and natural church.

Through significant natural detail, a redemptive image of physical healing, recovery from bereavement and natural therapy takes on still further resonances of, paradoxically, a pagan Christianity. *The Secret Garden* makes nonsense of Warnock's reductive caricature of children's books. And if one takes the figure of Ben Weatherstaff, his aged crustiness softened by delight in the children's health and energy, and sets him alongside 'old John with white hair', in Blake's 'Song of Innocence', 'The Echoing Green', not only the vision but the imaginative conception are seen to be virtually identical. Both *The Secret Garden* and 'The Echoing Green' (and many other poems by Blake) make readings available to children, and can enrich the imagination of both child and adult.

Imagination and its impoverishment are Warnock's true subjects. Having absolutely rejected the analogy between intelligence and muscle power, she only conditionally and reluctantly dismisses the analogy where imagination is concerned. 'Perhaps' it is nonsensical, and 'perhaps' is as far as she will go. What Warnock fears (her verb) is a corrosive adult habit of imaginative laziness, centred on these students, for 'if *they* are imaginatively lazy, who shall save the world?'

And here we come to the truth that lies behind much reductive adult comment on children's literature, and disparagement of adults who engage with it. Because Warnock is a philosopher whose tool is reason, we can see more readily when her subjective fears and prejudices take hold of it. All the fair-minded rational apparatus of 'Escape into Childhood' is an exercise not in reason but in rationalization, and what it rationalizes is the age-old fear of *trahison des clercs*. She fears an imaginatively lazy, self-indulgent and escapist adult intelligentsia, and is right to do so. Where she is wrong is in generalizing with such misplaced confidence about children's literature—both as a set of texts and as a source of readings. She attributes to it an imaginative restrictedness and simplicity which is not true of the genre but only of specific texts.

Adult literature has the same diversity of texts and readings. Would Warnock generalize about that in the same way? Of course not. She is wrong in building a generic frontier. And she is wrong in using and denigrating the word 'escape' to denote reading events which are almost always far more complex than she allows.

There would be cause for alarm about any adult who read nothing but children's books, just as there is eventual concern about a child who reads nothing but Enid Blyton, or one who reads nothing at all. The rational errors lie first in inferring static preference of reading choice (which is actually undesirable at any level of complexity and strenuousness) from diversity of reading choice (which is desirable at any level), and second in inferring a reading from a text read. Warnock's importance lies in valuing imagination as an indispensable faculty of the competent adult mind; but her students knew better than she did that for most people a nurtured continuity with childhood is essential to its wellbeing. Of course adults can be lazily escapist and children's books can service them; but children's literature can and frequently does replenish the completeness of a strenuous adult mind. Reading children's literature is often psychological re-reading of the self.

This practice of devaluing childhood and children's literature when we are really protecting our concept of adulthood (and exposing our unease about it) is extremely common in derogatory estimates of children's books. Mary Warnock's essay mainly attacks an adult readership, while Myles McDowell's 'Fiction for Children and Adults: Some Essential Differences' is a reductive categorization of the literature itself, but the attitudes behind them are very similar. McDowell's essay has also been influential and widely quoted, and I reproduce here the passage in which he summarizes the differences he perceives:

> . . . children's books are generally shorter; they tend to favour an active rather than a passive treatment, with dialogue and incident rather than description and introspection; child protagonists are the rule; conventions are much used; the story develops within a clear-cut moral schematism which much adult fiction ignores; children's books tend to be optimistic rather than depressive; language is child-oriented; plots are of a distinctive order, probability is often disregarded; and one could go on endlessly talking of magic, and fantasy, and simplicity, and adventure.

As soon as you say 'generally' and 'tend' you can assert almost anything while proving nothing much. Exceptions, however great, remain exceptions, so it becomes purposeless to note that *Silas Marner* and *Heart of Darkness* are very short, that Hemingway and many others employ dialogue and incident rather than description and introspection; that arguably conventions are much used in all fiction, and are often the prime

36

subject of fictional play; that *Middlemarch* develops within a clear-cut moral schematism; that Hardy usually disregards probability; and that one could go on endlessly talking of *The Magus*, and *Gormenghast*, and *The Old Man and the Sea*, and *Nostromo*. McDowell is listing expedient likelihoods, some of them questionable, with numerous exceptions on both sides of the invisible line. Differences of genre cannot be properly described in this haphazard way.

Behind the list, however, lies a chant not wholly different from Orwell's 'four legs good, two legs bad' in its meritocratic distinctions between the adult and the child. It runs 'Complexity good, simplicity bad; thought good, action bad; realism good, fantasy bad; idiosyncrasy good, predictability bad.' The point that matters is not that some of McDowell's distinctions loosely and broadly exist, as they undoubtedly do. What matters is that the process of transition from child to adult, as commonly interpreted from the fictions which adults give to children, is represented as development from a norm of short-term physical activity to a norm of long-term psychological activity, and from free to socially disciplined imagination. In fact, this is more true of critical valuations of adult life than of observable adult life itself. McDowell admits this in a significant parenthesis (my italics):

> The peculiar variety of emotional response [in a fictional character] simply isn't conceptually accessible to children (*and perhaps, in fact, to many adults*), and the reason is that the average child has not reached, until the mid-teens at the earliest, a sufficiently advanced stage of conceptual maturity to understand . . . such a condition.

McDowell is not wrong in seeing childhood as developmental (though I believe he devalues its autonomous intermediate states). The problem with his analysis, as with Warnock's, lies not so much in their conception of the child as of the adult. In many such accounts there is embedded an implicit mental picture of childhood as a gradual, steady climb towards a plateau of achieved maturity. The child's task becomes

37

the physically active one of seeking to understand the revealed landscape and his own relations to it.

There is in my view no wonder that we misunderstand the literature if we so misrepresent life itself. To understand the child's climb we must take account of all the pauses for breath, the sliding back down bits of scree, the numerous picnic places and bivouacs from which the child too examines the landscape, finding it sometimes marvellous and sometimes horrible. To understand the adult's plateau we must see that it undulates, has knolls and dips and sometimes chasms, that you must fight against a gale to keep your footing. (Some people find a hollow and just sit there.) Occasionally you climb back the way you came, either to shelter from the wind or to see the lower slopes again more closely, although they will not look the same as they did the first time, for you bring down with you your knowledge of invisible horizons. And often, very often, you climb down to give children a hand on the rough bits. The literature, and our readings of the literature—both as children and adults—reflect this irregular journeying.

Many of the features pointed out by commentators such as Warnock and McDowell are not in fact peculiar to children's literature, or to ways of reading it; the most they do is to indicate why a particular body of literature is likely to be owned or co-owned by children. Among the gathered characteristics of children's literature and of immature reading taste suggested by these critics, there are in fact three which are common to both these studies and call for comment: a taste for fantasy rather than realism, a liking for simple or definite or strong plots, and the prominence of child characters.

Only if these features are themselves oversimplified does there seem any reason why the maturing reader should outgrow them. As we grow up we are likely to find complex social realism more interesting, to complicate our sense of story and lessen our dependence on linear sequential action, and be chiefly concerned with adults just as children are with children. But such developments are not dismissals. We should still find that fantasy, like many other nonrepresentational forms of art, illuminates the real; that a good story is still a good story, and reflects the linear eventfulness which is truly part of life; and that the child within us stays for many reasons interested in children, most usually because we have some of our own. Only the presence of the child protagonist, I would argue, is characteristic of children's literature as a genre.

In all these three matters the needs and interests of most authors (whether novelists 'for' children or not), and of adult readers, and child readers, meet in a body of texts and blur the lines between children's literature and the rest. On the matter of story, here is J.B. Priestley, writing in a 1931 preface to a reissue of his first two novels:

> ... my conviction that the novel demands some sort of objective narrative. I still believe that a novelist should tell a story, and if possible a fairly shapely one, no matter how strong his subjective interests may be. Indeed, I consider this problem—that of combining a reasonably clear-cut narrative, in which may be found definite characters and scenes, with these subjective interests, this flickering drama of the mind and soul—easily the most difficult problem a modern novelist is called upon to solve. You may dodge it, of course, by simplifying or eliminating your subjective stuff, and thus bringing out a plain tale.

Quite simply, there is nothing immature or 'childish' about wanting novels to tell stories, and nothing artistically naive or passé in choosing to write one. It is a commonplace now that many authors write for children because the world of the adult novel is ideologically unreceptive to their narrative preferences, and that many adults read children's books because there, and only there, they find a well-told tale. These days, if like Othello you 'will a round unvarnished tale deliver', your best hope is children's literature. But to be successful in it you must have other qualities of imagination, defining centres of interest, as well as a gift for story.

Many years after Priestley, and in the age of literary theory, we would now assert that a novelist cannot simplify or eliminate his or her 'subjective stuff': that you may wish to tell an unvarnished tale, but there is no such thing as a plain one. In this respect children's literature and adult literature are alike. Even in its most unsophisticated forms, the children's book cannot wholly exclude what Priestley beautifully calls the 'flickering drama of the mind and soul', even if the author is intent on doing so. If we think it can be excluded, we have ignored, as many commentators do, the complexity of simplicity and the coded intricacies of language. Unlike Priestley in 1931, we now have no excuse for such ingenuousness about language and narrative. This has always been true if only quite recently understood, but it is also true that children's literature in the postwar years, growing steadily in artistic confidence, has engaged more openly with the 'flickering drama of the mind and soul'. Exercising artistic autonomy in the ways that Ransome and Townsend and Lewis suggested, writers have raised the stakes and found that many children can respond. So it becomes steadily harder to find narrative grounds for distinguishing between children's and adults' fiction.

Some fine attempts at formulation have been made, and a classic one seems to me that of Jill Paton Walsh in her essay 'The Rainbow Surface':

> The children's book presents a technically most difficult, technically most interesting problem—that of making a fully serious adult statement, as a good novel of any kind does, and making it utterly simple and transparent. It seems to me to be a dereliction of some kind, almost a betrayal of the young reader, to get out of the difficulty by putting down the adult's burden of knowledge and experience, and speaking childishly; but the need for comprehensibility imposes an emotional obliqueness, an indirectness of approach, which like elision and partial statement in poetry is often itself a source of aesthetic power. I imagine the perfectly achieved children's book something like a soap-bubble; all you can see is a surface—a lovely rainbow thing to attract the youngest onlooker—but the whole is shaped and sustained by the pressure of

adult emotion, present but invisible, like the air within the bubble.

This is splendid, but the fictive procedure so described is not unique to children's literature. The children's text will exhibit these qualities because it cannot otherwise retain its mature integrity and still be open to its audience. The adult text may work in the same way, but need not. However, some of the greatest texts and greatest writers do. Compare with Jill Paton Walsh the narrator's statement in Conrad's *Heart of Darkness* about Marlow's storytelling methods:

> The yarns of seamen have a direct simplicity, the whole meaning of which lies within the shell of a cracked nut. But Marlow was not typical ... to him the meaning of an episode was not inside like a kernel but outside, enveloping the tale which brought it out only as a glow brings out a haze, in the likeness of one of these misty halos that sometimes are made visible by the spectral illumination of moonshine.

We do not have to make the mistake of identifying Conrad with Marlow, or wholly fuse outer narrative with inner narrative, to see that this is nevertheless tantamount to artistic self-description, fully borne out by the rest of Conrad's work whether it includes Marlow or not. Some of our greatest novels work within the narrative constraints of children's literature; the difference is that they do not have to.

The case for fantasy is only one form of the case for imagination generally. Fantasy is one of many literary forms through which imagination is exercised. It has a certain kinship with some forms of scientific hypothesis, for instance, the conjectural totalities which astronomers and archaeologists sometimes infer from limited data and evidence. All are experiments with possibility. They are not more 'imaginative' than good naturalistic fiction or empirical observation and analysis, and the fantasist, the archaeologist and the astronomer can all be wildly fanciful, using masks of objectivity to disguise subjective purposes. But properly exercised they are all a disciplined quest for understanding, like the experiment with gender possibility in Ursula Le Guin's *The Left Hand of Darkness*. Of course fantasy (like imagination generally) can be used for escapist motives, but this is a feature of particular writings and readings, not of the genre itself.

Fantasy needs little defence, but I can move to the third and crucial characteristic, the child protagonist, by citing a fine doctrinal statement by Ursula Le Guin in which fantasy and childhood are combined:

> So I arrive at my personal defence of the uses of the imagination ...The children's librarians I have met seem to be what they are and to do what they do just for this reason, that they have not denied their own childhood. They believe that maturity is not an outgrowing, but a growing up; that an adult is not a dead child, but a child who survived. They believe that all the best faculties of a mature human being exist in the child, and that if these faculties are encouraged in youth they will act well and wisely in the adult, but if they are repressed and denied in the child they will stunt and cripple the adult personality. And finally they believe that one of the most deeply human, and humane, of these faculties is the power of imagination.

Just as the taste for story and the enjoyment of fantasy as part of 'knowing through imagining' are places where novelist, adult reader and child reader can meet in a text, so is a common recognition of childhood's significance. Many kinds of interest in childhood meet in children's literature: the child's concern with the presentness of her own childhood, and interest in its possibilities; the adult's recall of childhood and desire to refresh the roots and keep a sense of continuous identity; and the adult's hopes and beliefs and desires about childhood, what it is and what it ought to be. Child characters are only a part of this. In his excellent study *The Discovery of Childhood in Puritan England* C. John Sommerville emphasizes the particular interest that reform movements, such as the Puritans', show in childhood:

Reform movements provide excellent histories in which to look for an interest in childhood ... When people organize for change in this way, it is never long before they recognize that the rising generation will be crucial to their enterprise ... Also, the image of the child will inevitably figure in the movement's ideology, because all such ideologies include a particular understanding of human nature ... The modern-day continuing interest in childhood might be seen as reflecting our condition of "permanent revolution"—which will end when we despair of efforts to change the world.

Among so much that proves to be common ground between children's literature and literature generally, the complex preoccupation with childhood is the distinctive feature and special area of critical interest. Yet our evaluation of this important literature seems to me to be often conducted in ankle-chains because we lack a necessary item of vocabulary. The result is problematic judgements such as I have considered here. In the next chapter I shall propose the word that might meet our needs.

3

Childness and Youth

Ursula Le Guin noted that 'all the best faculties of a mature human being exist in the child', and it is important that in our thinking about children and their literature we should give due weight both to the differences between child and adult and to the similarities and continuities that link us all. In his study *The Use of Imagination* William Walsh observed:

> It must ... be remembered that psychological study has developed in such a way as to be concerned almost exclusively with the differences between adults and children. The similarities occupy only the tiniest part of its attention. Because of this we are immensely impressed with the uniqueness and autonomy of childhood, so that in a sense all our psychological knowledge has led us to think of childhood as a different and peculiar state, almost as something remote and alien to us.

Not only is our sense of difference profound—so much so that it colours our literary judgement, causing us to merge our concept of the literature with our concept of the child—but it narrows and polarizes our available vocabulary for describing child behaviour. We use 'childhood' as a neutral term for early human development. In the process we come to associate major development of all kinds with physical development, and instead of recognizing that it is lifelong we internalize the crude 'climbing to a plateau' image which I described in the previous chapter. 'Childhood' also becomes vaguely loaded with the freight of all the qualities and limitations which we associate with children, drawing them from our individual experience and our common culture. Novels for children incorporate these qualities and limitations, variously arranged and disposed. Because 'childhood' also does service as a neutral biological term, our objectivity and subjectivity are hopelessly confused. And we are inclined, as Walsh points out, to highlight differences at the cost of all we share.

When we come to the available adjectives, the problem of linguistic poverty is more obviously acute. The choice lies between 'childish', which is a term of disparagement even when applied to children (see again Peter Banning's 'Stop behaving like a child!'), and 'childlike', a word denoting innocence and naiveté which we use with condescending approval. (We would not care to be thought childlike ourselves.) And naturally enough, since the tautology is obvious, this adjective is rarely used about children. Something is amiss with our vocabulary when our only adjective to describe children being children is one of disapproval. The alternatives from other roots are little better. 'Juvenile' is also a reductive term, and children's books are critically downgraded when called 'juveniles', while 'youthful', which is a beautiful word but covers more than childhood, is mostly used as neutrally descriptive.

One of the deepest truths of language is that we cannot *mean* things unless we have the words to mean them, and in relation to childhood we are linguistically deprived.

In Act 1 Scene ii of Shakespeare's *The Winter's Tale* Polixenes, king of Bohemia, is speaking to Leontes, king of Sicilia, about his son:

> If at home, sir,
> He's all my exercise, my mirth, my matter:
> Now my sworn friend, and then mine enemy;
> My parasite, my soldier, statesman, all:
> He makes a July's day short as December;
> And with his varying childness cures in me
> Thoughts that would thick my blood.

'Childness' is a rare word in English. The *Oxford English Dictionary* gives it two meanings:

— childish humour, childishness
— child quality, being a child

Quoting Shakespeare's usage above, the *OED* also gives another instance, taken from George Macdonald's *Unspoken Sermons* (1884): 'Childlike enough to embrace a child for the sake of his childness.'

We can note with sympathetic exasperation that neither Macdonald nor the *OED*'s lexicographers were able to unshackle themselves from the existing adjectival vocabulary ('childish', 'childlike') in seeking to clarify a noun which patently means something different. Although Polixenes is referring, wholly without disparagement, to what might be termed 'childish humour', what he clearly means is the *OED*'s second usage, which is free of adjectival contamination: 'Child quality, being a child'. And it is something he prizes, as does Macdonald.

Polixenes speaks of 'varying childness'. His son Florizel's behaviour delights him by its caprice and changeability, as the boy tries out numerous adult roles in play. I have earlier referred to constructions of childhood, and argued that children themselves construct their childhood. This is what Florizel has been doing: experimenting with his identity through interaction with his father in diversity of play. This is a model of what children are doing in most of their activities, including reading children's books. (Adults can go on doing so, to their benefit, if they avoid enslavement by habit and routine.) 'Childness' in Florizel (and for Macdonald, and for the *OED* in its best efforts) is the quality of being a child—dynamic, imaginative, experimental, interactive and unstable. It is by our childness that we grow.

It is also by our childness in adult life that we remain, in Le Guin's term, the 'child who survived' and replenish our mature selves. If we turn from Florizel to Polixenes, child to adult, son to father, we can see that for Polixenes, and for Leontes also, childness has other qualities. Polixenes speaks for many adults, and for many authors and readers of children's literature, when he says that the child 'cures in me/ Thoughts that would thick my blood'. Florizel incites Polixenes to play, which all balanced adults need to do: we are playing when we tell or read stories, write or read novels, no matter how complex or mature or painful they may be. (Often we are also working without knowing it, as are children when they read. Children's literature rests on the principle that much play is inadvertent work, and work at its best is inadvertent play. So does adult literature, though in adult life less harm is done if the principle goes unrecognized.) In playing with Florizel, Polixenes is not ceasing to be an adult; he is not playing as a child plays, any more than adults read as a child reads. But there is a transaction between them, a shared set of pleasuring beliefs about childhood and child behaviour, in which the adult can engage—in our contemporary phrase—as a participant observer. The freshening perspectives this affords to Polixenes can 'cure' him of the mortifying effects of age. (We see in miniature here the magical process of secular redemption through children which is the central subject of Shakespeare's late romances.)

What Florizel and Polixenes share, in fact, is 'childness'. For the boy it is the presentness of his condition; for Polixenes it is participant reconstruction, made up from observation, and play, and memory, and values and hopes which he invests in childhood and the future represented by his son. Childness, the quality of being a child, is shared ground, though differently experienced and understood, between child and adult.

I wish to argue here that childness is the distinguishing property of a text in children's literature, setting it apart from other literature as a genre, and it is also the property that the child brings to the reading of a text. At its best the encounter is a dynamic one. The childness of the text can change the childness of the child, and vice versa. On other occasions of reading the encounter is only a mirroring, conservative and confirmatory: the child finds in the text a childness which largely reflects and duplicates his own. Such encounters are not valueless, far from it. Children cannot live all their lives in states of dynamic interchange; they also need the reassurance of staying put. However, it seems to me that as soon as we introduce the concept of childness into our reading of children's literature, we are better placed to understand the interplay of author, text and child. Also, we are better placed to see that readings of children's literature are a microcosm of the vaster social process by which children learn and grow.

In the speeches of Polixenes and Leontes in *The Winter's Tale* we can see the several elements of which adult childness is composed. The consolation and pleasure which Polixenes derives from his son's many-sided childness is accompanied by a sense of childhood innocence, and of adult life as bringing with it a fall from grace. Of his childhood friendship with Leontes, he says:

> what we changed
> Was innocence for innocence; we knew not
> The doctrine of ill-doing, no, nor dreamed
> That any did.

Our modern adult sense of childness is unlikely to be so gullible as to childhood's innate sinlessness; ours is the age of *Lord of the Flies*. Childness is a changing, culturally determined concept, not a static one, and this is very important to our understanding of its influence. The childness prevalent in our age will permeate the images of it which we transmit to children, in children's literature and in other ways. Polixenes believes not only in a kind of original innocence, namely that original sin corrupts us only with the knowledge of it, but also that childhood innocence is pre-sexual in nature, a belief that modern psychology has taken from us by its demonstration of infantile sexuality. We cannot now see childhood as Polixenes does. The childness which we find embedded in children's texts (and elsewhere) is a complex amalgam of more or less permanent characteristics with many changing ones, determined by religion, society, culture and science as well as being coloured by the idiosyncrasies of individual perception.

This raises a point which is crucial to my whole discussion, and again it is one which is illuminated by children's literature rather than peculiar to it. Because childness is the property of a text (as of many other adult constructs for children) and also a property of the child reader, and the reading event is one of many possible events when they meet, we are in serious difficulties if at any period there is a gulf too wide to be easily bridged between the childness of adult constructs and the childness of children. We are in trouble if there is a gap between what adults 'know' about childhood and what children 'know' about childhood, especially as adults and children alike regard such temporary, socially conditioned 'knowledge' as immutable and permanent. In the case of children's literature, it means that children will find books irrelevant, or silly, or untrue, and will therefore reject them, just as other parts of life will be rejected also. Likewise, if the childness of adult constructs in fiction and elsewhere is bewilderingly inconsistent, or contradictory, or incompatible with the perceived reality of the world that children experience most forcefully, then we can hardly be surprised if we find that children are disorientated, rootless and confused.

I propose 'childness', therefore, as a critical term with wider relevance. For the child, childness is composed of the developing sense of self in interaction with the images of childhood encountered in the world (including adult expectations, standards of behaviour, grants of privilege and independence, taboos, goals, and offerings of pleasure). For the adult, childness is composed of the grown-up's memories of childhood, of meaningful continuity between child and adult self, of the varied behaviour associated with being a child, and the sense of what is appropriate behaviour for a given age, of behavioural standards, ideals, expectations and hopes invested in the child as a child. For the child, childness includes the knowledge and acceptance that one *is* a child; for the adult knowledge and acceptance that one isn't, though adults have differing beliefs and valuations about possible survival of the child in the mature being. This compound of cultural and personal attitudes is articulated in a text of children's literature, and the *event* of children's literature lies in the chemistry of a child's encounter with it.

No word in current regular use denotes this 'child quality, being a child' in all its intricacy. Certainly 'childhood' itself does not. And with our two adjectives, 'childish' and 'childlike', we are still worse provided. The embarrassment of the word 'childish' is long-standing. Alexander Pope, writing about Ambrose Philips in the eighteenth century, made an eternally valid point and at the same time showed up the troublesome word:

Gay is writing tales for Prince William: I suppose Mr Philips will take this very ill for two reasons; one that he thinks all childish things belong to him, and the other because he'll take it ill to be taught that one may write things to a child without being childish.

Even reputable modern children's authors and artists remain defensive and unconvinced on this point, so that even the most effective and useful formulations are tied by the vocabulary. Peter Hunt notes that 'In essence, childhood is defined in terms of seriousness—hence the concept of "childishness".' That is, to be 'childish' is to be 'un-serious', and the adjectival resource belittles the person. R.D.S. Jack refers to 'the belief that those who write for children in whatever fashion are, themselves, childish'. Joan Aiken neatly made the point I have suggested in querying the 'plateau' image of adult life, and pointed to the developmental inconsistency of grown-ups: but she is still caught—to her evident impatience—by the word:

Obviously, writing for children is regarded by society as a fairly childish occupation. But then it occurred to me that most people's occupations are pursued at a number of different levels—at varying mental ages. A man runs his business affairs with a fifty-year-old intelligence, conducts his marriage on a pattern formed when he was twenty, has hobbies suitable to a ten-year-old, and a reading age that stuck at Leslie Charteris. Is he an adult or not? And if he is not, how would you classify his reading-matter?

Varying childness is complemented by varying adulthood, a fact which adults blushingly evade. Unfortunately the alternative adjective really is no help, as is apparent in this valiant effort by Madeleine L'Engle to explain why she writes children's books:

> Here are two words that may provide a key: childish and childlike. Just as there is all the difference in the world between a person who is *childish* and a person who is *childlike*, so there is all the difference in the world between a book that is *childish* and a book that is *childlike*.
>
> A childish book, like a childish person, is limited, unspontaneous, closed in . . . But the childlike book, like the childlike person, breaks out of all boundaries.

The definition of 'childish' here underplays the usual severity of the term. The childish person is generally regarded as selfish, petulant, frivolous, irrational and emotionally immature—that is, as combining a feature intrinsic to childhood by any definition, namely that of natural and blameless immaturity, with a collection of features associated with both children and adults at their worst. L'Engle dilutes the harsher word, but she also sentimentalizes the alternative. Certainly there are examples of pristine visionary insight which we might call childlike in a wholly approving sense: they would include those of Blake, a writer of children's literature, and Bunyan, who wrote poems for children as well as *The Pilgrim's Progress*. But the term is a difficult one, and is commonly used to suggest a harmless but limiting ingenuousness unlinked to special insights. We can think of modern children's books which fit the available meanings. A number of Enid Blyton's books (though not by any means all) are childish in the regular harsh sense, while Antoine de Saint-Exupéry's *The Little Prince* is childlike, having the quality of imaginative expansiveness which L'Engle seeks to make the word responsible for. One sees what she is driving at, and recognizes the distinction. But the two words are not satisfactory to describe the bulk of children's literature, ancient or modern.

Again it is revealing to find that the language contains another word which, like childness, is rare and out of use. In drawing attention to it, even so astute and sensitive a historian as C. John Sommerville is unable to detach it with sufficient confidence from the words we are lumbered with. He is making the important point that in our understanding and treatment of children we are not so superior to former ages as we would like to think. (Keith Thomas, disputing the theories of Philippe Ariès, has made a similar point.)

> Pollock does not attempt to explain a rise of affection or interest [in children] because she sees no evidence that they have, indeed, risen appreciably in the past several centuries. There was more affection in past times than literary sources have indicated, and there is probably less of it now than we would like to imagine. "Childish" is just as pejorative a term today as it was in Chaucer's day, and "childlike" was just as endearing a term then as now (though before Shakespeare's time the form was "childly"). Ambivalence is apparently a constant feature of attitudes towards children. Values have changed, to be sure, but that does not mean that treatment has improved . . .

Sommerville's account is scholarly and brilliant: I shall soon have cause to quote him again. Our complacency about the modern status of childhood is tellingly rebuked by his analysis. But in recalling for us the word 'childly', he too is entangled by modern vocabulary. 'Childly' is not a synonym for 'childlike', at least in the sense in which the current word is ordinarily used—with endearment perhaps, but also with patronage.

The *OED* is more helpful with 'childly'. It gives:

— Of, belonging to, or natural to a child or childhood; childish

— Becoming or proper to a child (as related to parent); filial

If once again we ignore the compulsory ineptitude of 'childish' (since even the arbiters of meanings are restricted by those we have), the beauty and aptness of 'childly' are clear at once.

This is an adjective closely linked with the noun 'childness' as I have traced it to its residual historic meanings and sought to amplify them for our current needs. In particular, 'childly' comprises within itself both the description of naturalness—of what is usual and normal in all children—and the description of fitness—the general perception at a given time of what socialized and educated children should be like, and what we hope they will be like. Consciously or unconsciously, these two concurrent meanings find their way into the childness which is expressed by adults in children's texts. (And once again, they find their way into other adult constructs for children.)

Whether or not the word itself is in current use, children meet in their everyday lives, in books and elsewhere, current adult concepts of childness, current understandings of what it is to be childly. As I have sought to argue, all such concepts will include aspects of personal memory and individual preference, so the terms cannot be reduced to a simple dialectic. But most children's books will embody a childness which includes both an implied sense of the natural and an implied sense of the ethical: an implied psychology and philosophy of childhood. Each of the two terms will differ in meaning from author to author, adult to adult, and child to child; and the balance between them will also vary sharply from text to text. But the doubleness of meanings is intrinsic and diagnostic, and we are deeply handicapped in discussing children's literature (and educational processes of which the literature forms part) if we do not have terms to encompass it. They exist in the language, and are unused.

The fact that 'childly' is unused tells us something about ourselves. Consider the group of related word-formations which end in the suffix '-ly'. 'Manly', 'womanly', 'godly', 'heavenly', and of particular interest in this context, 'gentlemanly'. These are difficult words now, because some of them have sexist connotations which were uncontroversial in the culture that produced them, but now irritate feminist critics and those sympathetic to them; others are Christian terms in a secular age; and 'gentlemanly' can be seen as archaically snobbish. What matters, however, is that they are all terms of approval, properly understood, and that they combine, as 'childly' does, a sense both of the natural self and the self which is socially admired. To be womanly is to be sexually natural in your behaviour and also to embody the approved ideals of your sex; and the same applies to the others.

Now consider the word-formulations which end in the suffix '-ish'. 'Babyish', 'womanish', 'girlish', 'devilish', 'hellish', and also, interestingly, 'churlish'. These are terms of disapproval, and they combine, as 'childish' does, a sense both of the natural self (as judged by the user of the word) and the self which is socially despised. In religious terms, '-ly' is reserved for God's domain and '-ish' for Satan's. In terms of social hierarchy, '-ly' is reserved for gentlemen, not to mention kings and princes, and '-ish' for churls. This group gives feminists a cause for justified fury. Whereas 'girlish' is a term of abuse, 'boyish' usually suggests in-dulgence. 'Mannish' is a cruel term for sexual incongruity, whereas 'womanish' is a milder term of behavioural reproof, and so on. It is quite clear that 'childish' is the opposite of 'childly', and that 'childlike' and 'childly' are not synonyms. (Compare the very different suggestions contained by 'gentle-manly' and 'ladylike': the first is fully invested with inward qualities of character and ethics, the latter with external man-ners and behaviour.)

It surely tells us something about our historical and current attitudes to children that we have kept the disparaging word 'childish' in full working order, while consigning the approving word 'childly' to the obscure recesses of the OED.

Our words, as I say, are our meanings, and there is more in-volved here than lexical exhumations.

Contrary to what we like to think, the closing years of the twentieth century are not the best of times to be a child. We might compare our present situation with the world in which Arthur Ransome wrote for children, in the 1930s and 1940s. Those were decades of material hardship which fewer children in western societies now face, and the children in Ransome's books (even the Coot Club) belonged to privileged sections of society and were quite untypical of most. The bullied deckhand in *Peter Duck* is an unusual reminder of a possible East Anglia which had not moved all that far from *Peter Grimes*, but Ransome's world has few children like him.

Moreover, we have seen already that Ransome denied writing with an eye to real child readers in the first place. He was, he said, just lucky because children liked what he did. We can be very sceptical about this. Like many children's writers, Ransome is probably being disingenuous in disclaiming any thought for actual child readers, whether he realized his duplicity or not. The illustrations he drew for the *Swallows and Amazons* series were avowedly intended to give the illusion of being drawn by his child characters, which hardly suggests a self-sufficient artistic aloofness. What I think Ransome means, and what many other writers mean, is that the child narratee is only part of the childness which they are investing in their books. The rest, in Ransome's case, was compounded from memory of childhood holidays, from the continuity through childhood, youth and adult life of his delight in sailing, from friendship with and observation of contemporary children (the Altounyan family), and from ideals of child behaviour and the process of maturing through responsible play. 'Better drowned than duffers. If not duffers, won't drown.' These are the raw materials of a complex construction of childness. What Ransome means by his denial is not that his child readers do not matter to him, but that in the last resort some things matter more. In the end, children must take it or leave it.

And, of course, they took it. Ransome's success is a matter of publishing history. The children who took it in the 1930s and 1940s included thousands who would never set eyes on a sailing dinghy, let alone own one. In Ransome they found far more than wish-fulfilment and escape, and no pretext for discontent and envy. For thousands of children in vastly differing circumstances, Ransome gave story form to a childness that spoke with their own. No doubt it had to do with independence, and self-reliance, and gang solidarity, and holidays, but more deeply it had to do with what it felt like, in that culture, to be a child, and revealed a community of childness which overspilt social and material boundaries.

A useful example of this is *The Big Six*, which must count as one of the most incompetent detective stories ever told. The Coot Club are unjustly accused of vandalism, when someone goes around loosing boats from their moorings. From the first chapter it is perfectly obvious who the real culprit is, and it takes over three hundred pages to expose him. But this is not the book's real subject. At its heart is the universal experience of being unfairly accused of a crime, of failing to persuade friendly adults of your innocence, of being thought to transgress standards that you passionately hold. The Coot Club's parents are torn between worryingly plausible evidence and defensive belief in their children, rooted in values which the generations share. The Coot Club know who they are and what they stand for, and the book's suspense lies in their desperate efforts to prove their loyalty to a binding social code. And Ransome's readers understood.

The books are still in print, are sold and read, even though they are dated in many ways and are twice the length of modern children's novels. What keeps them alive? The childness of Ransome's books is far removed from most current images of childness that children meet. Are the books kept on a life-support system by the nostalgic memories of bookish modern parents? Are they part of a modern ghetto of literacy, very sizable and commercially viable for publishers but still a minority? Do they therefore belong to an insulated community of children for whom Ransome's childness can still compete with all the pressures to reject it? Or is it possible that some children still meet in Ransome a world of childness which, if not providing the common ideological ground that it once did, nevertheless represents what they secretly desire and prefer? And where do these readers come from? Are they widely dispersed as they once were, or do they come from homes which offer (like the Coot Club parents) antiquated forms of family back-up?

Such seemingly improbable survivals give cause for hope that lines of communication are still open. But evidence suggests a period in which the gulf is widening between the childness of the book (along with other encounters with imaginary children) and the childness of the children, and one in which the secure parental background of the Ransome world has less and less in common with the modern child's experience. The subliminal ideologies of children's literature are part of a much wider world. All writers for children embody patterns of childness in their texts, whether or not they set out to, but to most writers for children the childness of the child, the childness with which they hope to negotiate, to work a chemistry of the imagination, must seem increasingly out of reach.

There are many reasons for this, among them the rapidity of change in children's environments, so that even young writers for children are prematurely obsolete in their personal inheritance of childness; and the mass of contradictory signals which children now receive, attempting to define their childness for them, as compared with the relative uniformity of earlier decades; and the defictionalizing of childhood itself in favour of fictions for immature adults. Earlier uniformity can be exaggerated, but comparatively it did exist, and what mattered was not that it was ideal, but simply that it was uniform.

In her essay 'Looking at Children: The History of Childhood 1600 to the Present', Christina Hardyment, while rightly acknowledging that modern childhood is far from a doomsday scenario, nevertheless pointed to some of its worrying features, which centre on the weakening of the family unit. She stresses the change in the child's role from contributor to consumer in the economic ethics of family life. ('Childhood is now an experience of consuming food, clothes and entertainments manufactured outside the home and bought with their parents' hard-earned cash, rather than a matter of learning about and contributing to a busy centre of production.') Parents, most significantly mothers, are now distracted by activities outside the home ('"emotionally unavailable" is the chilling phrase coined by the newly fashionable family therapists'). 'Images of anxiety are a recurrent theme in modern paintings of children.' And most important of all: 'Perhaps the greatest single difference between childhood in the past and in the present is the strange lack of self-confidence that marks modern parents; the absolute decline of their authority.'

This is borne out by a recent study of 20,000 children aged eleven to fourteen, the results of which were reported in *The Sunday Times*:

Today's schoolchildren are a distressed generation: alienated, anxious and addicted to television ...

John Balding, director of Exeter University's schools health education unit, which carried out the study, said parents often appeared 'frightened' of their children. 'They don't know how to give them adequate direction. In order to escape from this, they try to make their children grow up too quickly and put the responsibility for their actions into the child's hands...'

It leaves children 'robbed' of their childhood, according to Robert Whelan, of the Family Education Trust. 'They are being thrust from childhood into a spurious adulthood,' he said. 'Why can't they enjoy being young for longer and do things that all youngsters used to do?'

In the reading events of children's literature the childness embedded in texts transacts with the childness of the child, and in present-day society this crucial transaction appears to be socially endangered, not only in the field of children's literature but more widely.

In the world of children's reading, transactions of childness with childness are imperilled not just by resistance to reading or competition from the media, but for other serious reasons, notably the erosion of confidence in the status of child and parent. The historian Hugh Cunningham compares the past with our present situation:

[in the past] Parental power determined how children were reared. In the late twentieth century, however, matters are different. Adults portray the world external to the home as full of danger, and seek correspondingly to protect their children by denying them autonomy. At the same time, their confidence in their own authority has been weakened by a variety of factors—commercial, legal, psychological—which make it difficult to carry out that protection as they would wish to. The result is that, to a much greater extent than in previous centuries, child-rearing has become a matter of negotiation between parent and child.

Many children's books set out to reflect the new situation. Gone are the days when children were freed for adventures because Daddy was skippering a cruiser or running an Oriental tea plantation. The feckless parent who appeared some years ago in John Rowe Townsend's *Gumble's Yard* is now widespread, either absent or inept, as in Janni Howker's *The Nature of the Beast*, and often far more childish than the child, as in Nigel Hinton's *Buddy* and Theresa Breslin's prize-winning *Whispers in the Graveyard*.

Since it is absurd to suppose that we can dismantle technological advances in the media and reverse social trends in treating and defining childhood, there is a present duty upon writers for children to re-imagine childness. The formidable task in which the writer shares is to present a meaningful childness to the child while still engaging openly with present-day realities. To re-imagine childness cannot involve suppressing memory, or the child in the self, or the ethics of personal growth, because these are what energize the writer's imagination and make it live. All writers have personal agendas; so do all critics, teachers, social workers and psychoanalysts; it is unavoidable, however much it may be disguised or denied. Writers are no more subjective than others who deal with children. But these irrepressible subjectivities will be sterile unless they search actively for contact with the childness of modern children. Since the task is enormous, I suppose what I am saying is that we need a generation of great children's writers, who can find new and imaginatively authentic expressions of childness. Even then, literature is a minor component of any child's experience.

One thing literature can certainly do is to revive the lapsed concept of 'youth'. Our present need is to reaffirm the double truth that Walsh pointed out: children are separate from adults but also like us and continuous with us in the pattern of human life. In negotiating childness we can find common ground, but only if children themselves freely recognize it. In thinking of youth we look at the actual years we share, when child and adult are actively alive together in the individual. 'Adolescence' is not a synonym for youth: it denotes a narrow band of tempestuous sexual awakening which has social and emotional consequences. There is more to youth than that, and youth lasts longer, if we understand it to be closed only by full entry into adult life. In youth we are finding out more about ourselves than just our sexuality, and we can be well into our twenties before the process is over. To find it reflected in story, we can usefully think not of 'teenage fiction' or 'novels for young adults', but of a 'literature of youth': a body of texts to rub shoulders with children's literature, and the texts can be very great ones.

The argument I have been advancing depends on an acceptance that childhood is not a fixed concept nor one on which we ourselves hold special and terminal wisdom, but rather one that fluctuates with historical process and will continue to do so. A minor distinction of children's literature, alongside its main one of helping children to grow, is the accurate fossil record it provides of adult beliefs and attitudes, past and present. This is especially true of the relation between childhood and youth. C. John Sommerville again supplies a valuable link between us and the seventeenth century:

Childhood, as well as Puritanism, requires definition, since the Puritans and their contemporaries were rather inclusive, not always distinguishing childhood from youth. This was not because they recognized no difference, but because they did not see growth as the discontinuous process described in modern developmental stage schemes. To them childhood was a more gradual and even a longer process. Leaving home for domestic service or apprenticeship did not end childhood; in certain ways it did not end until marriage and household independence . . . This may . . . provide us with new considerations in our own views of the boundaries of childhood.

In the topsy-turvy world we now present to children, supposedly mature adults often impose a premature adulthood on children (if only in the entertainments they think fit for them). They do so in order to evade responsibility, and so expose their own childishness. The media confirm this paradox of inversion. Christina Hardyment shrewdly observes:

> Children are portrayed as making a better stab at growing up than adults in films such as *Parenthood* or *Look Who's Talking*. The child stars of television series such as *My Two Dads* and *The Wonder Years* are far more streetwise and competent than their parents.

If we take our cue from the Puritans and rethink our sense of childhood and youth, we may come to realize that to accomplish adulthood is a long and complex process, which few of us achieve with lastingly secure consistency. To 'keep the child in ourselves' is not an eccentricity of children's writers but the common human lot, so we had better try to do it intelligently.

A literature of youth can show us the significant experiences which both consummate our early life and enable us to leave it behind. They are the times that Conrad referred to when he said 'Only the young have such moments.' In Chapter 7 I shall look at presentations of two such experiences which have major fictional expressions and unusual symbolic force. But since we seem never to leave childhood wholly behind, or do so only at our peril, we must next look briefly at the process of memory itself, which is a major part of our childness and the special province of the children's writer.

4

Memory and Narrative:
The Children's Book as Autobiography

So far we have distinguished two essential properties of children's literature. One is the quality of childness, in which the writer's memory of childhood plays a major part. The other is interest in story, and in linear narrative. Neither of these is unique to children's literature. Childness is the central imaginative interest of a literature of childhood, some of it meant for adults and embracing child readers only by chance; it includes *David Copperfield*, and *A Portrait of the Artist as a Young Man*, and *What Maisie Knew*. Linear narrative in the forms which give pleasure to children and to children's writers also drives the major adult novel in many of its guises, especially in the nineteenth century. In this section I wish to look more closely at memory and at linear narrative, to see if they have special meanings for the children's book, and to ask whether they are separate or connected.

We have plenty of valuable evidence in the form of statements made by writers themselves about their work, and one of the most revealing is Catherine Storr's in her essay 'Why Write? Why Write for Children?' After publishing a children's book early in life, there was an interval during which she qualified as a doctor. She asks why, when she began to write again, she returned to the children's book instead of writing for adults :

> First it was obviously tempting to continue in the field in which I'd made a start. Second, by the time I was writing again ... I'd got children of my own to whom I was telling stories ... and some of these stories seemed to me worth writing down. These I consider quite respectable reasons. The third, which is less so, is my own

remaining childishness. For years I wouldn't admit this, although I knew I wrote my best books not for my children, but for myself. William Mayne, when asked once for whom he wrote his books, said, 'For the child I once was'; I'm sure this is true of many writers for children, but I think it is also true that one writes for the child one still is. Lastly, I've continued to write for the young, not only long after I should have ceased to be childish, but also after my children were grown up, because of my lasting need for the story form.

By now I need scarcely point out the obstructive presence of the word 'childish'. Using it in quest of honesty, Catherine Storr is forced by it to sound apologetic. If the words 'childness' and 'childly' were substituted (and they are what the author really means) the need for apology would disappear. We should be left with two intrinsic motives: the need to connect one's lost childhood with its surviving presence in the self, and the need for 'the story form'.

But what are novels for adults if they are not stories? They are certainly narratives: *Ulysses* and *The Tale of Peter Rabbit* have this in common. *Ulysses* is also a story, but in a refined, almost self-disqualifying sense of that word. Often the postmodernist novel, though undeniably narrative, can hardly be said to be 'story' at all. Children's literature can in fact be said to be (chiefly) the beneficiary and also (in small ways) the victim of developments in modern fiction for adults and in modern criticism. One reason why children's literature has been taken more seriously in the last twenty years is that 'narrative' is no longer a dirty word for academic critics, and instead a major concern. All narratives, from the most apparently simple to the most intricate, are relevant to the theorist's interests. On the other hand, the conceptual distinction between 'narrative' and 'story' is still a confused one. 'Story' can still seem like a denigrated junior partner in this duo, though less denigrated than in days when it stood alone. Simultaneously, the postmodernist adult novel has actively repudiated linear cohesion in narrative as a falsification of experience, leaving the inherited structural positives of logic, pattern, order, meaning, closure, to popular fiction such as detective stories and to children's literature. Children's literature itself has moved towards postmodernist practices, notably in picture books and young adult novels, but much less commonly in mainstream stories for middle childhood. The effect has been to win for children's literature an expanded adult readership among people who want linear narrative and find good children's books more imaginatively stimulating than formula fiction for grown-ups. The question I wish to ask is whether a liking for story (by implication unsophisticated) is all there is to it.

Here is another key statement to clarify the issue, this time by Jill Paton Walsh :

> . . . many contemporary writers, myself included, write for children not because we are interested in children—though of course, on the side, some of us are—and not at all because we wish to shape, influence or educate anybody; but because our aesthetic preferences, our character and temperament have led us to like the sort of literature that children also like, or are thought to like, even if it is a kind of literature that is disdainfully thought of as *childish* [my italics] by the modish and intellectual among our contemporaries. It is my strongly held opinion that the kind of book I try to write, and which many of my contemporaries write brilliantly—the fine 'children's book'—can be written only by people who like that kind of thing for itself, and for themselves, and do not see it as any kind of come-down or any kind of educational tool. If they have had a good grounding in English Literature, for instance, the chances are they will like border ballads and carols better than court poetry, medieval narrative poems better than Spenser, Shakespeare better than Jonson—well, that one is fairly usual, after all!—the *Odyssey* better than the *Aeneid*. The thing has, in short, a discernible aesthetic . . .

She goes on to describe the adult readership of the fine children's book:

Some of these adult readers, avid and enthusiastic as they appear to be, do not read much contemporary adult fiction. Even more of them read only books from other lowly categories: science fiction, detective stories, romances and historical novels. The serious novel seems to say nothing to them at all. They are not unliterary . . . They are the missing mass audience that sustained the novel of the last century, and has been lost in ours.

Both Storr's and Paton Walsh's statements were published in 1975, and much has changed since then, along the lines I have described. The note of artistic apologia is muted now, though conversely something of the confident imaginative energy has been lost. What matters here, though, is the emphasis on narrative of certain kinds, on a distinguishing aesthetic, and one which cannot be identified with simplicity. Shakespeare is not simpler than Jonson, nor the *Odyssey* than the *Aeneid*. The difference between them is that they incline towards different hypotheses of possible order, which dictate different needs and methods of aesthetic patterning, and the whole is rooted (Barthes or no Barthes) in differing make-up of the constructed authorial self. The need for story and linear narrative, which happily coincides in certain adult authors and readers with almost all children, is not an immaturity or intellectual inadequacy, reducible to silly caricature by academics. It is neither more nor less than a construction of the self in the world.

There seems to be a serious difference of emphasis between Storr and Paton Walsh. Storr openly acknowledges the importance of her childness: the past child as a living agent in the adult self. Paton Walsh disclaims interest in children as a factor in her writing, except in a community of aesthetic taste. No one who reads her work, however, could possibly deny the importance to it of memory, and of—in the title phrase of Ian McEwan's splendid adult novel—the child in time. What seems to matter most to Paton Walsh and her fellow writers is not so much (or only) the child, but a philosophy of selfhood based on patterning and memory (in which childhood is an indispensable continuing event) expressed through an aesthetic of linear narrative (which children like, and which squares with their provisional, evolving organization of relations between themselves and their worlds). The two elements of memory (as an essential part of childness) and of linear narrative are therefore indissolubly linked.

To substantiate that point, I wish to cite Mary Warnock's study *Memory*, a vastly more considered and helpful work than her article discussed earlier. In writing about the processes of memory, the literary form that occupies her is naturally autobiography rather than fiction—and certainly not children's fiction—but the connection she makes is crucial:

[Recollection] is an active and creative undertaking. It is the reconstruction of a life in which episodes are fitted into a whole. If it gives pleasure, the centre of that pleasure is the sense of continuity between then and now which makes the story one, and mine. It is, of course, easy, at times, to deny such continuity . . . The self *then* may seem so unlike the self *now* that it may seem tempting to say they are two different people. In such a mood, a mood of rejection of his past, a man may say that he now has nothing to do with that other person, the person who figures in that 'scene'. But, if he says this, he deceives himself. If he can reconstruct the scene in recollection, not simply knowing that it occurred, but in the crucial way knowing what it was like, then he must also know that he was that person, and that there is a causal continuity between him (his body) then, and him (his body) now. To understand his continuity, to grasp his own duration is to defeat time, for he has not finished with his past. It, with his present, together make the pattern. *The plot embraces them both* [my italics].

In Warnock's view there is a natural and profound human need to establish the continuity of our individual lives, to maintain an unbroken line of connection between our past and our present. At some level this impulse and this need do indeed seem to be intrinsic to the motivation of our most distinguished children's writers. Moreover, it seems to be closely linked for many authors with a need to maintain continuities which go beyond our personal histories and include the history of our families, our birthplaces, our homelands, our cultures and our races. Concern for such continuities is evident in novels which celebrate continuities linking old and young adults across several generations, such as Lucy Boston's *The Children of Green Knowe* and Penelope Lively's *The House in Norham Gardens*. These and many other books are explicitly acts of praise for memory. Clare in *The House in Norham Gardens* consciously stores impressions of her great-aunts in her mind, like a squirrel storing nuts for winter, ready for the future years without them. Not only are such novels celebrations of contact between living generations, but evocations of a living past made unified and still accessible by continuities of blood and place and culture.

Many historical novels for children (more so than those for adults), and above all the ubiquitous fictions of time travel produced over the last century, are inspired not by love of the past for its own sake, not by interest in its differentness, but much more by the process of transmission and continuity, the subtleties of kinship between dead and living, and the features of hidden resemblance which underlie surface change. These processes are analogous at deep levels with the continuity between past and present in our individual lives, and above all between our years of childhood (which for the author are dead and gone just as the Elizabethan age is dead and gone) and the child who lived those years, who survives in our memories and present consciousness like our historical and cultural inheritance from the sixteenth century.

As Warnock sees it, for a man to 'understand his continuity, to grasp his own duration is to defeat time, for he has not finished with his past'. She is thinking of the autobiographer, and through him the ordinary man or woman, for whom these are in her view natural needs. For the children's author, for whom they tend to be especially important, it is usually the roots of life in childhood, its significance in our sense of personal time, which drive the imagination, but this is only an expression of a general human need for continuity which children themselves experience from infancy. Construction of the self in time begins very early and is lifelong; it is not a question of adult immaturity or nostalgia. In the negotiations of childness which occur between author and child reader in a text of children's literature, the adult author is in some measure living life backwards to enable the child to live it forwards; the author is reconstructing her childhood, and in so doing is helping the child to construct hers. I do not suggest any altruistic educational intentions on the author's part: there seems little need to question the assertion of so many authors that they do what they do to please themselves. What matters is the way this pleasing of the self occurs, and the happy coincidence that allows it to please children.

The pleasure for children lies first of all in linear narrative. Warnock explicitly makes the connection between memory or recollection and 'plot'. Elsewhere in her book she notes, 'We turn our life into a story by remembering it, and any story, or history, is thus timeless; we can tell the story to ourselves again and again, and the truth it contains does not change.' The last part of this formulation seems to me dubious, and in the following discussion I shall seek to qualify it. But the central point is very important. The natural procedure by which we establish the continuity of our individual identities is by linear story. We all do it, including children. In adult life it is possible for us to construct our selves, and our interpretation of experience, in ways which complicate the linearity or even abandon it entirely. But for the author such as Catherine Storr or Jill Paton Walsh, who seems to stand for a more general adult inclination, linear story of particular kinds is the aesthetic mode of expression for a philosophical conviction and a psychological need. Their work is a complex and unique expression of a simple and general desire. It generates children's literature in their and other cases because childhood is fundamental to their personal sense of identity in time, and their books construct it by literary means that are accessible to children.

*

For the modern theorist, critic, and 'serious' adult novelist, this is mere pretence and illusion. There is no such cohesion of personality or continuity of selfhood as is postulated here; these are mere fictions, ways of managing the true fragmentation of personality and experience. There is no absolute measure, whether we call it God, or time, or self, or fixed linguistic meaning, to which we can anchor existences that are always engaged in self-dispersal. There is no author present in a text, no language which provides a common currency of exchange between mind and mind. It is not the man who in Warnock's account disclaims connection with his past who is deceived, but Warnock herself, and linear narrators along with her. Identity is a fiction, and generates self-delusive fictions to support it. Common sense may tell us otherwise, but common sense is no yardstick for truth; common sense once told us that the sun went round the earth.

There is much that modern theory can do to illuminate children's literature, but there is also no question in my view that much contemporary theory is hopelessly incompatible with the very concept of a 'children's literature', and with what authors think they are doing when they write it, and what children appear to be doing when they read it. If some modern commentators are right, we are all playing meaningless games. If on the other hand a philosopher such as Warnock is right, with her belief in logic and in rational common sense and in defined terms and fixed meanings and words such as 'memory' and 'imagination', then neither the genre nor the critical discourse which affirms its existence is based on self-deception.

To make sense of the transactions of children's literature—their meeting-ground of childness in the writing and reading of texts—it is necessary to agree broadly with Warnock's position but take issue with particular simplicities in her account of it.

The proposition that we construct our selfhood through memory, that we depend for our identity on our sense of personal continuity in time, and that we express this to ourselves by storying our lives, seems fundamental. Almost all people, including children, act on these suppositions, and would find it hard to manage without them. If they are deceptions they are necessary deceptions, just as belief in God is either true or a necessary deception to countless millions of people. Our need for story is arguably not only a need for escape and entertainment but a need for analogous imaginary patternings which reinforce the constant work of storying our own lives: we need stories as we need food, and we need stories most of all in childhood as we need food then, in order to grow.

Effective writers of children's literature are often those who retain this childhood intensity and urgency of storying, whose childhood is alive in memory and present existence because it is still essential to their mature procedures for articulating the self in time. Because this is a mature need, there is nothing inherently childish about it. Childishness is a possible element in authorial childness, and certain highly successful children's authors are in some ways childish, but childishness is not a diagnostic quality of children's literature, whereas childness is. Unless the author's childness is active in a text, that text is not children's literature in the sense I defined it earlier, and a sense of personal existence as a lifelong story is essential to it. (This is not a question of nostalgia: a writer's personal history may be rooted as much in deprivation, unhappiness and loss as in remembered pleasure.) It seems likely that people choose to write for children, or find that their books are children's books, because these origins and continuities of self excite their imagination more strongly than they do for other writers, and release an appropriate aesthetic of literary method. Probably they find their many adult readers among people like themselves, with comparable mature interests and needs.

In matters of continuity and narrative, therefore, Warnock is largely right. Where she is wrong is in her excessive faith in precision and fixity, both of memory and of linguistic interchange. For children's literature the importance of this is that negotiations of childness are more fluid and creative both for the adult author and the child reader than some tempting fixities make them seem.

Warnock said of memory and narrative: 'We can tell the story of ourselves again and again, and the truth it contains does not change.' This supposes that memory itself is constant—that the childhood experience I remember next year will be identical with my memory of it this year, and it will therefore mean the same to me. Against this I would place a passage by the American scholar Paul John Eakin, in his study of autobiography, *Touching the World*:

My view of the self and its history, developmentally considered, would be something like this: I would begin by acknowledging the fundamental reality of difference, of instability, of discontinuity in human experience, positing a self that is constantly changing and evolving. But I would argue that the serial, potentially fragmentary content of this model of life history is radically altered by the functioning of memory, which supplies the possibility of identity otherwise lacking in the biography of the self. In this view memory would be not only literally essential to the constitution of identity (we need think only of the consequences of amnesia) but also crucial in the sense that it is constantly revising and editing the remembered past to square with the needs and requirements of the self we have become in any present.

This view accepts the discontinuous nature of existence as we find it reflected in much modern theory and fiction, but also accepts that we need and achieve a sense of identity. We do this through a constant dialogue between experience and memory, in which *both elements are unstable*. We construct our personal continuities but we do not remain the same people: we evolve. Only by memory can we cope with our own personal evolution, but memories are not constants: we revise and alter them to fit our present needs.

I find Eakin's view convincing and helpful. It tells us something about the children's writer, who typically uses childhood as a crucial reference point in storying, habitually citing it as important both in motives for writing and in thematic preoccupations. Memory of childhood is one element in a story's childness, and we can see that for some writers the image of remembered childhood apparently survives intact from book to book whereas for others it undergoes deep change. (Consider, for example, the evidence of revisionist memory between *Tom Sawyer* and *Huckleberry Finn*.)

More importantly, however, Eakin tells us something about child readers and the likely place of fictions in their lives. Children evolve fast. They face discontinuous experience more sharply than adults do. Notoriously, they revise their memories with exceptional aplomb and imaginative zest. Fed by memory, experience and imagination, their sense of identity and of childness, of what it is to be a child and what it is to be a particular child, is volatile, experimental and creative. To be 'a child in time' is a turbulent experience. Children cope with it by making life into a story, a story both continuous and ever-changing. As all this goes on, the stories they read and hear expand the fund of personal experience and give it anchor points, at once fixed vicarious memories and fixed vicarious futures, which can be read, and often re-read and re-read, and subtly, unconsciously revised as life goes on and identity evolves. A story *seems* fixed, but is not: and that, especially in childhood, is the particular glory of those texts we value most and carry forward into adult life.

This points, however, to Warnock's second dubious fixity, that of language and text. She notes (again of autobiography, but this creates no problem because the writing of autobiography is a fictive act):

> If something is known directly, recalled vividly, by an author, then *my* imagination can cause *me* to grasp that very truth, through *his* described memory of it. His imagination and mine show the universal in the particular.

Questionable assumptions lurk in this. There is the supposition, queried above, that memory is stable, the truth of experience being accurately reflected in the memory of it. It is taken for granted that language can act as a transparency, through which the reader receives what the author supplies.

There is the assumption that imagination is a precise instrument of understanding. And there is finally an implication that memory and imagination are almost interchangeable terms, whose encounter in two minds reveals an objective general truth.

Current literary theory would repudiate virtually all of that, and so would my account of children's literature. Language is coloured by complex patterns of individual association. We can share it well enough for general agreement but not, except in highly controlled contexts such as law, for contractual exactness. Literary works allow many readings, and children who do not decode some demonstrable linguistic subtleties of a novel have not necessarily failed to read or understand it. Warnock is right to suggest that imagination is the province of the reader as well as the writer, but since imagination is by any definition a creative faculty, not merely a cognitive one, it follows that every story is re-created by each of its readers, including children. It is interesting that Warnock finally seems to accept memory itself as creative, and therefore has some common ground with Eakin; most children's writers would wholeheartedly agree with that. Lastly, the reading of fictions (and of autobiographies, which are fictions) does not produce immutable general truths, but personal truths which are likely to resemble each other.

Although these points are true of all readings (except those subject to specialized encodings), they are notably true of children's literature because of the gaps in age, experience, linguistic competence, developmental need, and above all else perhaps in concepts of personal time, which separate author from reader. I have argued that the reading encounters take place in a field of negotiation called childness, to which writer and reader bring different kinds of expertise. The writer's childness is composed of memory, and in Storr's phrase 'the child one still is', and observation, values, sympathies and desires, but never temporal presentness. The child brings the experimental volatility I have described, in which memory also plays a part, and a highly creative one. The common language of author and reader is not so much language as linear narrative itself. Story *is* language, one which adult and child are good at sharing.

In the light of the argument in this chapter, I should like to quote some of the statements made by children's writers about the motive of their work. We have seen one category earlier, represented by Ransome, Townsend and Lewis ('you write the best book that is in you', 'the best art-form for what you have to say'), and another category is represented by Storr and Paton Walsh ('children's literature' gives hospitality to an aesthetic which values story and linear narrative). The third category of voices in the artistic confessional is probably the most numerous. It includes Catherine Storr, who writes for the child she was and still is, and William Mayne, whom she quotes as writing 'for the child I once was'. Nina Bawden said, 'The child I am writing for is, I suppose, the child I used to be.' Ivan Southall said, about the time when he found his true vocation with *Hills End* and *Ash Road* : 'I felt that I had become a child again, that I was writing *out* of my own childhood, and that the standards of maturity were necessary only as a filter of the most superficial kind.' Alan Garner said he was writing 'to make myself live the life that in some way I was prevented from living as a child.'

There cannot be mere coincidence in such widespread community of purpose. These writers are unanimous that 'the child I once was' is the child they are writing *for*, not the one they are writing *about*. The past self is important not so much as protagonist (idealized or otherwise) but as imaginative receptor, and what is happening is a kind of displaced autobiography-through-story, ministering to exactly that need in childhood for story as imaginative self-aggrandisement which I discussed above. One senses in many writers an unstable ideal of *wholeness* in child experience, a profound sympathy with deprivation or one-sidedness, or incompleteness of physical, emotional or imaginative life. In some respects *The Secret Garden* is the archetypal children's book.

Among modern writers the most precise self-analysis of all, perhaps, is Rosemary Sutcliff's:

When people ask me, as they quite often do, whether I find it easier to write for children than for adults, or which I like doing best, or what is the difference between the one and the other, I have always claimed that I do not write for children at all, but simply for myself. More accurately, I suppose, that I write for the small private pocket of unlived childhood within myself which I am sure is to be found in many, if not most, children's writers. My pocket was unlived (can one unlive a pocket?) because I spent a large part of my childhood being ill; Kipling's because he spent several years of his being desperately unhappy; Beatrix Potter's because much of her youth was a wilderness of loneliness.

Many of the considerations raised in these pages are just as true of popular, critically vilified authors like Enid Blyton as they are of the distinguished novelists I have quoted. Sometimes the childness of a novel is partial, limited, even obsessive. Often, as I suggest in talking of wholeness, it reflects, endorses and encourages the essential many-sidedness of growing up. Children take from a story what they want and need. In doing so, they may through vicarious experiences be filling up pockets of hitherto unlived childhood in themselves.

5

Signs of Childness:
A Summary and Critical Approach

Childness, as I have defined it in preceding chapters, is a composite made up of beliefs, values, experience, memories, expectations, approved and disapproved behaviours, observations, hopes and fears which collect and interact with each other to form ideal and empirical answers to the question 'What is a child?' As you would expect with an amalgam drawing on such diverse sources, both public and individual composites of childness are rarely simple and coherent, and the institutions which embody them—families, schools, legal procedures, children's books—are not simple and coherent either, but full of inconsistencies, strains and unspoken priorities. Childhood itself, the first phase of childness, is constantly interacting with empowered adulthood, the second phase of childness, and the chemistry of that interaction at any one time determines the success or failure of adult–child relations. Children's literature is one such field of interaction.

In this chapter I shall suggest a representative set of questions to disentangle individual strands that go to weave the composite of childness, first treating literature only as a minor element in a much larger pattern. I shall then suggest some features of the encounter between the childness of individuals and the childness of texts. Lastly I shall suggest some literary questions which might clarify the childness of the books we present to children.

THE DIVERSITY OF CHILDNESS

Is childness a fixed and permanent composite? No, it is extremely flexible, and is historically, socially and culturally determined. In individuals it may change radically with personal experience, and for children themselves it inevitably undergoes profound changes as they grow up.

Example. In Britain and in western societies as a whole today, there would be general agreement that childhood is a period of economic dependency, given over to physical, emotional and intellectual growth through education and play. As a state of economic dependency (if not in other ways) it lasts well into the teens, and during this period it is right to place strict legal limits on the kinds of work, and amount of work, that children can do for money.

This is not a model of childhood, and hence an element of childness, that would have been recognized in the nineteenth century, after the Industrial Revolution. Nor would it be recognized today by the child carpet-weavers of India, the boy soldiers of Liberia, the boy coal-miners of Colombia, or the child prostitutes of Thailand.

Is childness a detectable feature of nations, or social groups, or individuals? All three. In some nations and societies at some times, there is a very powerful consensus on the rights and duties of children, the precise duration of childhood, and the values and expectations set on children. This is still true, for example, of many contemporary Asian cultures. At other times nations may embody many different attitudes in groups, social classes, and individuals, and these differences may cause political and social tensions for adults, and social and psychological tensions for children, especially when the law is far apart from perceived realities. The childness of a country at a given time is affected by its degree of consensus about childhood, and the strains and dissents which pull against consensus.

Although a national childness affects children, in most societies they are more directly affected by the childness of localized social groups and institutions, above all their families, but also their social class, their ethnic group, their religions or lack of them, their peer groups, clubs, schools, and gangs. These more immediate influences in their lives may present a unified or at least fairly consistent image of childness to the growing child, or may send out contradictory and incompatible signals. The groups with whom the child has direct contact may also be in harmony or disharmony with the composite childness which the child meets through films, television, electronic media, and books.

Most important of all, all individuals develop their own childness from a very early stage of childhood. It will be affected by the national, social and family composites set out above, but also by individual experiences and memories. The childness of individuals may be complex, highly conscious, and a very important element of daily life, or it may be relatively simple, largely unconscious, and at most a sporadic feature of everyday existence.

Example. The childness of a secondary school teacher who is also the mother of children aged seven and three will be very different in complexity, consciousness and importance from that of a childless male tax inspector. However, this is never a question of having composite childness or not having it. We all have it, by virtue of the fact that all of us are or have been children, and carry our childhood experiences forward into adult life, where they react with our observations, and knowledge through the media, of contemporary children.

Just as the childness of nation states (in terms of values, beliefs and expectations) can change over time, so can that of individuals, in the light of perceived changes in child behaviour (real or imagined) since the adult was himself or herself a child.

Example. One might ask, 'Is there good cause to be afraid of children?' In Britain, likely answers to this question have changed over the last ten years, especially during the 1990s. A few years ago, almost everyone would have assumed that the only people with cause to be afraid of children were other children. In the mid 1990s this is no longer so. Many parents, teachers, neighbours and old people are afraid of children, often in the case of parents their own children. Public reaction to some crimes committed by children is evidence of intense and widespread unease. There is a deep desire to label certain child offenders as monsters of evil, and hence by reassuring inference exceptional and rare. As with other such phenomena of childness we may find this fear beginning to be reflected in children's literature, and more conspicuously in novels for adults about childhood. See, for example, J.G. Ballard's *Running Wild*. And more conspicuously still in certain films and videos.

SOME ELEMENTS OF COMPOSITE CHILDNESS

What kinds of question contribute to concepts of childness? We derive our sense of childness, which is partly conscious but largely unconscious, from many sources, such as the above example of children as a cause for fear. What follows is only a selection from the many questions that we may pose (as a rule unconsciously, haphazardly and incrementally) in order to produce our composite—and often nowadays confused—formulations of childness. They include questions large and small, theoretical and pragmatic, metaphysical and psychological, objective and subjective.

Is the 'natural' child a noble and innocent savage or a brutal and dangerous savage? Or not a savage at all, but primally moral and hence virtuously innocent?

Is the effect of education and experience a corrupting one, or is it the purpose of family nurture and of education to socialize the child, displacing antisocial instinctive desires by habitual behaviour of a more civilized kind? (That is, how do we respond to Blake's dialectic between Innocence and Experience?)

How thick or thin is the civilized surface which children develop as they grow? Does the peer-group (or tribe) end anger the stability of individual socialized behaviour? (These are the *Lord of the Flies* questions, which are fundamental to modern visions of childness. They have found their way into

79

many modern children's books, for example Richard Armstrong's *The Mutineers* and Vivien Alcock's *The Trial of Anna Cotman*.)

Is the child a proto-adult, in linear development to maturity? Or is childhood a distinct and separate biological state, best seen as pre-human or potentially human? If the second is true, at what age, or stage of development, do children become recognizably human? (Richard Hughes's novel *A High Wind in Jamaica* is a provocative response to this question, deliberately explicit in its biological and psychological assumptions.)

Is the child gifted with qualities or insights that adults lose? Does memory of childhood therefore enable us not just to maintain continuity of identity but to recall an irreplaceable and trustworthy freshness of perception and spiritual knowledge? (That is, how do we respond to the childness of Wordsworth's 'Ode on Intimations of Immortality'?)

Do we expect children to be consistent and sequential or erratic and unpredictable in maturity of behaviour?

Do we believe that children are capable when necessary, even when very young, of understanding and coping with adult emotional crises and practical emergencies, or that such capability only comes when the appropriate age and level of maturity has been reached? Likewise, do we believe that children usually find the necessary resources of maturity to cope with disasters in their own lives, such as bereavement, injury or illness, or that premature exposure to such stresses can be permanently damaging?

Do we believe that children at quite young ages are capable of taking on adult roles, such as that of surrogate parent, and are capable of functioning safely, responsibly and successfully independently of adults, for example if normal parental care and control are taken away? (This falls short of the *Lord of the Flies* scenario, but is the subject of many popular and famous texts in children's literature, a notable example being Ian Serraillier's *The Silver Sword*. It also preoccupies the adult novel about childhood, such as Ian McEwan's *The Cement*

Garden.) If we take an optimistic view of children's ability to cope, at what age is it reasonable to expect it?

Do we believe that children are capable of reversing the normal adult/child roles, assuming leadership and offering protection to vulnerable adults if the need arises? At what age might they do so?

Are children capable of behaving better than the adults who surround them, of exercising moral autonomy, of setting an example, and if so can they do it without being conceited, humourless, priggish, or otherwise failing to be childly? (This question is especially prominent in relation to science fiction or dystopian narratives for children, such as Robert Swindells's *Brother in the Land* or Jill Paton Walsh's *Torch*.)

Conversely, do we find that in our experience children are subversive of idealizing stereotypes that adults cherish, and if so, is this a matter for regret, or neutral observation, or pleasure?

Do we believe that somewhere under the diversity of child experience there is a universal bedrock of common needs, desires and behaviour that we call childhood, or that everything depends on environment, experience and social conditioning?

Are children adaptable to a volatile and changing world in ways that adults are not, and are they therefore, rather more actively than the mere process of time and generational succession dictates, in the business of displacing the adult?

Are children in a perpetual state of friendly or unfriendly war with adults, declared or undeclared?

Do we believe that children have multiple selves, and that their behaviour and indeed personalities are likely to be significantly different depending on whether they are with siblings, with a peer group, with adults, or alone?

What sorts of behaviour do we associate with particular age-groups, and levels of maturity? Do we have age-norms, and what is our attitude when children behave, as we see it, precociously? Or retardedly? (That is, childishly.)

Do we have normative images of what boys are like, and what girls are like, and what the 'normal' behavioural differences are? Do we have unspoken, and perhaps unconscious, ideals of what the norms and differences *should be*? What for us is the baseline: what are the minimal acceptable differences that we will tolerate between the behaviour of boys and girls? Do we have different margins of tolerance where transgression of our norm is concerned, for example by demanding clear-cut demarcations of dress, speech and behaviour on public occasions or in public places that would not bother us in the privacy of home? How prudish are we in insisting that sexual differences should be kept respectably out of sight, and at what age do they start to be important? (Not, presumably, at birth! But how soon afterwards?) In these and other ways, how much does our composite image of childness, our answer to the question 'What is a child?' split automatically for us into 'What is a boy?' and 'What is a girl?'

Can adults (and *should* adults) establish confederate alliances with children, as if in conspiracy on equal terms, surrendering the privileges of adult status? Is it indeed possible to do this, other than by histrionics and deceit? And do children in our own experience welcome it? What relations of minimum psychological distance (not to mention physical distance) are permissible between the child and the parent, teacher, uncle, 'uncle', grandparent, guardian, or storyteller?

What kinds of behaviour are intolerable in adults but are accepted or at any rate recognized as natural in children? More difficult and sometimes more important, what kinds of behaviour are intolerable in children but are accepted or at any rate condoned in adults? In our sense of childness, do we press actual children into conformity with a theorized childhood?

When does childhood end? Is there one age when we would expect to start saying, 'Come on, you're not a child any longer,' or is there a set of different exit-gate ages for different circumstances?

Lastly under this heading, what do we remember of our own childhoods? Were we happy? Were we solitary or gregarious? Did we use story as imaginative escape from a painful or difficult reality? What were the key moments and key experiences, good or bad? What were the moments when we felt our world to move irrevocably on, leaving part of ourselves behind and ever afterwards out of reach? What did we miss? Among the things we missed, what matters still, and chafes our minds in our maturity? What are we still attempting to make up for, perhaps through our own children, perhaps through the children's books we write, or read?

THE CHILDNESS OF TEXTS AND OF READERS

In Chapter 2 I argued that a set of definitions of children's literature is available to us, and for the purposes of this summary they split conveniently into two essentials. Children's literature consists of *texts* and *reading events*.

For literary criticism it is usually the *text* that matters most. The critic's task is to determine the general features which distinguish children's literature as a genre, or sub-genre. This task is extremely difficult, because it is one that we must simultaneously perform and try to subvert. Throughout this study I have suggested that the boundaries between child and adult, children's literature and adult literature, are always simultaneously existent and nonexistent, real and unreal, precise and imprecise.

In her essay 'Escape Claws: Cover Stories on *Lolly Willowes* and *Crusoe's Daughter*', Lissa Paul attacked the reductive effects of generic categorization on children's literature, and continued:

Once we realize consciously that we've categorically *excluded* children's literature from literature, we also realize we've already made a tangle of assumptions about what's appropriate for a children's book and what's not. A happy ending? Non-sexist language? Characters who display the 'right' moral values? You may want to try to make your own list of the identifying marks of children's books. I disagreed with myself at every turn. Whether we like it or not, there is no such thing as separate but equal.

83

I would broadly agree with this, but would argue that there *is* such a thing as separate but not separate. That is, there are fairly precise ways of usefully elaborating the principle that 'a good book for children is a good book for everybody'. We can say of many adult texts that they are inappropriate for children, though I suggested earlier that many such texts may reach an individual child reader and so become not 'children's literature' but 'a child's literature'. However, we cannot say categorically of any children's book that it is inappropriate for adults (even if the appropriate adults are confined to the immature and the professional). I can call Shakespeare to my aid (as with the term childness itself) to express the doubleness of generic definition that I wish to argue for.

In *Troilus and Cressida* Troilus is taken by Ulysses to witness Cressida's unfaithfulness with Diomedes. The visible evidence of his lover's treachery is an intense psychological shock to Troilus. The faithless Cressida he is looking at both is, and is not, the Cressida he knows. And he says so: 'This is, and is not, Cressid.' The experience as an adult of re-reading a known and much-loved children's book can be the literary equivalent of Troilus's ordeal. Readers can actually feel betrayed. Short of that, they can certainly feel that they are not reading the same book. But they *are* reading the same prose sequence: it is not the text which has changed, but the reading event. 'This is, and is not, children's literature.' The difference lies not in the text, but in the reader, and in the reader's ability and readiness to locate the readings that the text makes available. Viewed in this way, children's literature both is and is not separate from adult literature. The differences which cut it off from the body of literature generally may be 'indistinct/As water is in water' (*Antony and Cleopatra*).

The concept of childness, and the distinction between texts and reading events, together provide the key to a clear discussion of children's literature and a critical procedure which recognizes its separateness *and* inseparateness from literature in general.

Everyone, including the child, has that body of feelings and beliefs about childhood which I have called childness. They vary from person to person not in existence but in complexity. Children's writers, by the very nature of their trade, are likely to have complex visions of childness, which they will invest in their writing whether or not they intend to. Some authors writing for an adult readership also write frequently about children and childhood, and invest their texts throughout or in particular episodes with intricate versions of childness. These may or may not attract the attention of some child readers. For the literary critic, analysis of the childness invested in such a text, whether or not it is officially designated children's literature, is likely to illuminate our understanding.

On the other hand, the fact that a book has child characters does not automatically mean that it presents a detailed construction of childhood or has a complex investment of childness. Some novels for adults make extensive use of child characters and yet display a very narrow and impoverished interest in children. They may, for example, use children merely instrumentally in order to exhibit features of the adult world. And curiously enough, the same is true of some children's authors. There are novels published as children's literature (and they usually include at least one significant child character) which embody only simple forms of childness and display a weak concern with childhood. They may very well succeed as exciting narratives and be highly popular with children on that account, yet offer limited resources for the kind of self-recognition and imaginative self-exploration which distinguishes a text of children's literature that is rich in childness. A classic instance of such a text is *Treasure Island*.

Conversely, a book may not include any child characters at all, and yet have manifest complex childness. (Some war stories, such as *Biggles*, may fall into this category, but the most important group are animal stories.)

Most interesting texts of children's literature will embody a significant investment of childness. Critics can usefully analyse them to expose, for example, their implied responses to the questions listed earlier in this chapter. We can ask ourselves,

'What images of childness does this novel make available to the child?' To see whether these images are likely to be accessible to inexperienced readers is also the critic's concern, and involves analysis of—for example—language, characterization, and narrative procedures. Henry James's *What Maisie Knew* contains an immensely rich and complex image of childness, but not one that is likely to interest a child.

The critic's concerns therefore include the ideological features of a text, its linguistic and narrative strategies, and hence conjectural reading events. Some form, however crude and simple, of this critical procedure lies behind such statements by reviewers as 'This book will appeal to twelve-year-olds.'

Outside the critic's compass lies the actual reading event, where children's literature shifts from text to experience. Since every single twelve-year-old reader will bring his or her own childness into dialogue and negotiation with that presented in books, and since every child's childness is necessarily unique, a multiplicity of readings will be generated. Some of them will give major educational opportunities to the parent and the teacher, but in the ideal situation of busy and varied reading activity, most will rightly be the child's own business.

A study of childness in texts may indicate the probable success or failure of reading events. In the list of questions directed at revealing unacknowledged childness, I included this: 'What sorts of behaviour do we associate with particular age-groups, and levels of maturity?' In recent years children have matured physically at an earlier age than they used to, and have also moved at an earlier stage from activities linked with childhood to those associated with adolescence. Partly under the influence of the media, commerce and marketing, and peer-group fashion, they have seemed to leave childhood behind much earlier. We may doubt whether external behavioural maturity is accompanied by the emotional maturity to cope with it, but it is still an observable fact of life. Increasingly children are prematurely wrenched from childhood by a drug culture or family collapse. When children of ten or eleven now meet children of ten or eleven in books, how does the childness of the book compare with the childness of the child?

Many fictional characters now seem very young for their age to contemporary children. When the book belongs to an earlier period, as Ransome's do, good readers are sophisticated enough to make allowances for such discrepancies and tolerate characters and behaviour which are out of sync with their own lives. When characters are supposed to be their own contemporaries, tolerance may be harder to come by. Writers who depict young people as today's young readers know them, in a recognizably tough world (as Robert Swindells and Melvin Burgess do), may be critically praised and yet dismissed by many adults as too controversial, because the approved childness of children's literature is in arrears of current street realities. I do not argue this to press the claims of brutal urban realism, but to suggest the risks for children's reading of a widespread mismatch between childness in the text and childness in the world. In her manual, *The Way to Write for Children*, Joan Aiken discussed the problems of the would-be novelist for teenagers :

> It is absolutely no use attempting a teenage novel unless (1) you are a teenager yourself and can speak with authority, or (2) you are in constant daily contact with adolescents, either parent, teacher, social worker, or psychiatrist, and consequently familiar with the language, problems, priorities, and complications of being a teenager at the present time.
>
> Trying to grope back to your own teens if they are more than five years removed will not do.

This seems to me quite true, and true nowadays for readers younger than the teens.

EXPLORING THE CHILDNESS OF TEXTS

What literary strategies does the writer employ to express childness? There is great variety in the linguistic and narrative procedures which writers use to express childness in their texts. Some are touched on in previous sections of this chapter. I propose others below, but again they are only intended as examples, not as a comprehensive list.

— Are the child characters psychologically realistic? Are some characters authorially preferred, by being given a sympathetic psychological realism which is offset against unsympathetic caricature for others? Is precision of individualized psychological portraiture connected or not with external social factors, such as social class, or race, or parental occupation, or region and hence dialect?

Example. An admirable instance of scrupulously balanced characterization despite differences of socially ratified dialect is the relationship between Andrew and Victor in Jan Mark's *Thunder and Lightnings.* Not all children's books observe the same high standard.

— Are the child characters differentiated from the adults, on a sliding scale from realism to caricature? There may be reasons, other than the author's desire to ingratiate herself with child readers, why differential characterization might be appropriate.

Example. A distinguished adult novel about childhood, often read in schools, is Susan Hill's *I'm the King of the Castle,* a claustrophobic novel about ultimately lethal bullying. The only major characters are two eleven-year-old boys, the mother of one and the father of the other. In the introduction to a school edition of her book, Susan Hill wrote: 'It [the novel] isn't really about their parents, Mrs Kingshaw and Mr Hooper. They are rather two-dimensional characters, and deliberately so; they are formalised even in speech-style (whereas the boys talk, I hope, as eleven-year-old boys do talk).'

Many children's texts reveal a very similar strategy, and for good reasons; but we should note that as in Hill's case it says something important about the author's conception of the possible separateness and insulation of the child's world from the adult's. It may also, again as in Hill's case, enable the author to indicate the relative vulnerability, loneliness and powerlessness of the child as compared with the adult. Or in other cases it may express an opposite view, where a conventional and two-dimensional adult character suggests a hidebound ineffectuality when set against adaptable and enterprising children.

— How are questions of gender, and gender relationships presented by the author? What gender roles and status are suggested, for example between siblings, between parent and child, between friends or within peer-groups? Is there any standard difference in the text between the kind of detail we are given about boys and girls respectively? (For instance, are we told what girls wear but not what boys wear?) How are responsibilities (active or passive) distributed between the sexes? Who takes the lead in conversations? Who has key ideas and generates initiatives?

Example. In *Swallows and Amazons*, when Titty is left on the island, note how the conventional female role of the passive, back-up, home-caring, nervously imaginative girl is established, confirmed and reconfirmed (by Mother's visit), and then triumphantly subverted.

— Is characterization consistent, with switches and inconsistencies of behaviour being plausibly accounted for, or is it arbitrarily subordinated to the conveniences of the plot or ideological purposes of the author? Most children are more volatile than adults, but only in degree. Random, expedient behavioural switches in child characters may suggest not only authorial laziness and incompetence but also a view of childhood itself, as psychologically unpredictable and only of short-term behavioural significance.

— Is the plot consistent, and intellectually coherent? Does the author play by the rules of the chosen narrative game, whatever they are? This is very important. It is an area where questions of literary genre and convention intersect with expectations of and assumptions about the child reader. For that reason, I give two problematical examples, covering three books.

Example 1. Conventions of time and magic
In Philippa Pearce's *Tom's Midnight Garden*, the story rests for almost its whole length on the apparent truth that Tom can

actually move in time, albeit as a 'ghost', to the lost Victorian garden of the house where he is staying. He meets the girl Hatty, and forms an important friendship with her. In the last stages of their supernatural defeat of time, Tom asks Hatty to hide a pair of skates under the floorboards of what in later time will be his bedroom. Returned to the twentieth century, he finds them there. As a 'given' of the narrative, Tom's actual transference through time is thereby a physically proven fact. However, at the end of the novel, when Hatty is identified with the aged and fearsome Mrs Bartholomew upstairs, it is suggested that Tom's and Hatty's time relationship is actually a phenomenon of dream telepathy, in which Mrs Bartholomew in her lonely old age dreamed of her past and Tom, in his loneliness, picked up the dreams and responded to them.

Myles McDowell, in the essay quoted earlier, speaks with amused condescension about the folly of the adult arguments which this incident causes. Children, he suggests, do not notice it or are untroubled by it. Certainly there are many children for whom the seduction of the story overrides the inconsistency, though I have also come across many who are puzzled and disappointed by it. However, if children's literature is children's *literature*, if it 'both is and is not children's literature', then *Tom's Midnight Garden*, which is an accepted modern classic, should not need to have such dubious allowances made for it.

In her conference address 'Time Present', reprinted in the volume *Travellers in Time*, Philippa Pearce gave her own account of the background of her narrative choices. She knew about and was impressed by the time theories of J. W. Dunne, especially his book *An Experiment with Time*. Dunne influenced many authors in his day, notably J.B. Priestley. Pearce is not sure whether she even understood his theories, but she goes on :

> But, in *Tom's Midnight Garden*, I wanted to bring those two childhoods—each to be as absolutely real as the other—together; and there had to be some rational justification. So I

adopted Dunne's theory—or seemed to. I think I must have felt a certain self-doubt in this, for I added the bolstering suggestion that dreams can work a time-shift. I also threw in an elaborate reference to Time from the Book of Revelation.

There is a casualness about this throwing together of 'rational justifications' which I find objectionable: it suggests an intellectual condescension towards the (child) reader not unlike McDowell's. One rational justification, chosen as a single narrative hypothesis for fantasy, is desirable though not absolutely necessary; any old rational justifications, thrown in for good measure regardless of consistency, are a different matter. Would Pearce have written like this for an adult readership?

However, I suspect that the imaginative and compositional truth is rather different. The Dunne-based theory of actual co-existent times, on which the narrative depends until the last chapter, entails a considerable investment of childness, a fictional celebration of authorial childhood memory and conditional belief in fantasy. The novel's intellectual world is the child's world, and obstructive adult rationality like Uncle Alan's is authorially impugned. In the last chapter, the adult world reasserts itself. Hatty is a lonely old widow, not a girl, and Tom has been reclaimed by the adult world of home and parents. What we find at this point is a withdrawal of authorial childness to match the events of the narrative; and an author suddenly embarrassed by the narrative apparatus she must present to the re-imagined grown-ups who (like time itself) have closed the party. The writer substitutes a final (Uncle Alan-like) psychological rationale for the quasi-scientific fantasy which the incident of the skates has 'factually' ratified and proved. This is an important example of fluctuating childness in a major text, and it damages the artistic integrity of the story.

Example 2. Conventions of death
Philip Pullman's *The Shadow in the Plate* (later revised and

reissued as *The Shadow in the North*) is the second in a series of melodramas set in Victorian England. The books seem to anticipate a teenage reader: there is considerable violence, to which the spirited and capable heroine, Sally Lockhart, contributes her fair share; there are backgrounds in business and finance; and there is sexuality: shortly before the end of *The Shadow in the Plate* Sally and her young partner, the photographer Frederick Garland, make love, and at the end of the book she is expecting his baby. This is the world of the melodramatic thriller, violent and sensational. When the reader is entertained by such a lurid imaginative scene, does *anything* pass muster in it? The test comes at the end of *The Shadow in the Plate*. Just after his one lovemaking with Sally, Frederick dies, killed in a fire which is due to arson on the part of a criminal enemy. He is a character we have grown through *two* books, the first of which ends happily, to like, admire and cast as the hero.

Though loosely categorized as teenage novels, these books appeal to younger readers. So they raise questions both about the childness of the text and of the reader. Neither death nor sex is any longer a taboo subject in the children's book: in these ways recent work has reconstructed fictive childhood, freeing it from a protective voluntary censorship which is out of line with children's knowledge and awareness. Our modern childness has rediscovered death, including children's deaths. The death of the *hero*, however, is more controversial. In this case there is literary convention at work, which in such melodramatic thrillers protects the hero and the heroine against all assaults of their enemies. In the first book, *The Ruby in the Smoke*, this convention is fully endorsed, only to be violated in the second. Consequently there is a literary question which concerns both the kind of book (the convention of melodrama) and the fact that the book is the second in a sequence which has seemed to set other, more reassuring rules, whereby hero and heroine go right to the edge, but not over it.

It can be argued, then, that Pullman is using literary means (the deconstruction of a literary form and narrative expectation) to reconstruct the childness of his implied reader—to redraw the capacity of young readers to accommodate dissident narratives. He can be seen to place the fraudulent fictive reassurances of 'happily ever after' against children's knowledge of an actual world in which injustice thrives and good people undeservedly die. The childness of these texts is not only one in which the author does not offer children any treaty of immunity, but one in which he *seems* to offer it, then cancels it.

Much the same is true of Sylvia Waugh's novel *Mennyms Under Siege*, the third in a sequence of five stories about a family of life-size rag-dolls, who by dint of tactical reclusiveness and much ingenuity and pretence contrive to live in pseudo-human normality in modern England. The series has been widely compared with *The Borrowers*, and is popular with quite young readers. One of the 'rules of the game' for the series has been that Mennyms, being dolls, do not die. (They do not eat, or feel pain, either, so they resemble human beings emotionally but not biologically.) At the end of *Mennyms Under Siege* one of them (arguably the most attractive) *does* die. This unexpected disaster can be defended as a narrative occurrence on the grounds that the whole conception has rested on recurrent intimations of mortality—not death exactly, but the dangerous longueurs of habit, self-destructive impulses to change, and constant reminders of insecurity and danger. Can children draw the analogy between life's echoes of death and death itself? I doubt it.

This is another instance of an imaginative conception breaking its own rules, again after earlier books have seemed to establish them. In this case the event is justified both artistically and as a transaction of childness because it draws on the implicit contractual understanding with the child reader that the family of dolls are *displaced* humanity. Just as a younger child knows that her doll 'is' human, but is also a toy, so the older child reader is likely to accept the convention that Mennyms 'live' yet do not live, and hence 'die' yet do not die.

In the next book all but one of the Mennyms 'die' and eventually come to life again. This is part of an uninsistent, subtle allegory about the plight of humankind, but it is made accessible—and its pains endurable—to the child reader because it shares in childness with the almost universal imaginative power of children to imbue toys with life.

Following on from these examples, what taboos *are* observable in a given children's text, and what forms of linguistic or narrative circumlocution and evasion are employed to keep them sacrosanct?

Who is the implied reader? Who is the *preferred* reader? Is there linguistic evidence that the book is addressed mainly to boys, or to girls?

Is the implied reader consistently a child? Or consistently someone who will not regard himself or herself as a child (and is not so regarded by the author) yet is demonstrably pre-adult? Or does the book adjust its implied reader as it goes along, perhaps intermittently confiding in, or sharing jokes or prejudices with an implied *adult* reader? (A classic example of this last occurrence is J.M. Barrie's *Peter and Wendy*, but it can be instructive to direct the question at C.S. Lewis's *Chronicles of Narnia*.)

Is the story told in the first person or the third person? From whose perspective is the story told? One, or more than one?

If the story is told in the third person, is the authorial voice omniscient, authoritative, and apparently impartial? If so, in what respects is its impartiality illusory or deceptive? What does it take for granted about the child reader? What elements of character and behaviour (especially in children) does it seek to persuade us are natural or unnatural, admirable or despicable?

If the third-person narrative voice is not (and not trying to be) impersonal and aloof, is it seeking to ingratiate itself with the child reader, and establish a conspiracy? If so, what construction of childhood does it align itself with, and expect to befriend? What characteristics which are known to be common in childhood, and supposed to be outgrown in maturity, does the authorial voice exhibit to strike up alliance with the reader? Spitefulness might be an example. Roald Dahl and C.S. Lewis are pertinent authors to consider here.

Does the authorial voice place the reader in an intermediate relationship with characters—for instance, by assuming in the reader a mature judgemental view of characters who are roughly his or her own age? If so, is a particular judgement urged, implied or assumed?

What is the linguistic relationship between dialogue and narrative prose? Are there differences in either or both, depending on whether or not adults are present? What do such differences (or the lack of them) suggest that the author believes about the separateness and autonomy of the child's world?

Is the child's perspective offset against others which place it— for example, the reported views of other children, or dissonances between children's intentions and the actual consequences of what they do, or between their emotions and attitudes and the social reality which is 'objectively' presented? Directly equivalent questions could be asked as an approach to *Hamlet*, but it is just as sensible and rewarding to ask them about a children's book.

Is the child reader offered any eavesdropping on adult speech and behaviour when no child is present, or is the child-perspective never broken?

What is expected (shown as normative) of children in the text, and what is expected (demanded) of the child reader? Are there significant differences?

At the end, has the child protagonist moved forward in any significant, sustained way, or do children relax (or relapse) into an earlier, less mature, perhaps more secure stage of development?

Through questions such as these, we can attempt to reveal both the childness of a text and the effectiveness of the literary procedures through which it is expressed.

6

Texts and their Childness

In this chapter I shall take just a few of the points discussed in previous chapters and develop them in a little more detail, in relation to particular texts.

CHILDNESS WITHOUT CHILDREN:
BEATRIX POTTER'S *THE TALE OF MR TOD*

The Tale of Mr Tod is an animal story and like Potter's work in general it has few or no 'human' characters—in this case none at all. This is one of the longest of Potter's little books, and has some of the *grand guignol* qualities of other Potter stories such as *The Tale of Samuel Whiskers*: it is a comic melodrama, a blend of farce and incipient horror, with an underlying satire aimed at human domesticity. There is something in it for every reader. Though nothing in the story excludes the child, there are linguistic and narrative features which seem to need an adult mediator first time round.

There is a double plot. In the framing plot, the offspring of Benjamin and Flopsy Bunny are abducted by subterfuge. Tommy Brock the badger takes advantage of the hospitality offered by the little rabbits' babysitter, their grandfather Mr Bouncer, and carries them off in a sack to eat for breakfast. When Benjamin discovers the fell deed, he bravely pursues Tommy Brock to get them back, helped en route by his resourceful cousin Peter. In the inner plot, Tommy Brock occupies a property which actually belongs to the fox Mr Tod, and there he goes to bed, anticipating rabbits for breakfast. Mr Tod, the housemproud possessor of several homes, indignantly attempts to evict the interloper.

Beatrix Potter is famous for introducing difficult words into stories for small children. Her description of lettuce as 'soporific' is always quoted. *The Tale of Mr Tod* is no exception: for example, Tommy Brock enters the rabbit hole 'with alacrity'. These ambitious linguistic excursions are not direct attempts to broaden the small child's vocabulary. Rather they are recognitions of the child's propensity to copy grown-up language and play games with it. Potter uses her own adult pleasure in language, especially its pompous and antiquated forms, to offer invitations to the child. 'You can master these words,' she says to the child reader, 'and in mastering them you can mock the silly grown-ups.' Her 'difficult' language is one means by which she allies herself with the child, always keeping her distance, always the authoritative storyteller, yet placing herself and the reader in a shared position of playful satiric adulthood. So there is a maximum of invitation and a minimum of deterrence when she says Mr Bouncer is 'stricken in years', or that Benjamin is 'the afflicted parent': the words mix together in shared amusement with simplicities like 'nice' and 'nasty', and colloquialisms like 'all of a twitter'. The game reaches its highest pitch of imitative pomposity in the judgement of Peter (that adventurous adult-child) that 'My Uncle Bouncer has displayed a lamentable want of discretion for his years.' How many small children in the last hundred years must have found a pretext to say *that* about somebody?

The language is one means by which Potter repeatedly invites the child into enjoyably superior positions vis-à-vis the 'adult' world. She often resorts to the dramatist's device of making the audience privy to information that characters do not share, and she also uses the dramatist's freedom to switch audience sympathy and viewpoint from one character to another. (This is easier in plays than in novels.) This 'play'fulness is one reason why generic terms such as 'farce' and 'melodrama' are especially appropriate to Potter. She is both storytelling and enacting a play for young readers, inviting them into a series of 'reader positions'. It takes little imagination to see how very close this is to the daily experience of early childhood.

The fact that all the characters are animals makes flexible child positions even easier to attain. In the framing story there is no doubt who the villain is: it is Tommy Brock. The negligent Mr Bouncer is the disgraced adult who is also the naughty child (and is punished near the end when Flopsy takes away his pipe and hides his tobacco). The child enjoys the humiliating demotion of adulthood, but only when its consequences are known not to be disastrous: Benjamin is already rescuing the babies. Before that, Tommy Brock, with his constant dangerous grinning, is a real threat to the baby rabbits (whose state of help-lessness the reader has already outgrown). The reader is in a superior position to the victims, and can adopt the quasi-parental role of Benjamin, the actual parent, in pursuing the affably murderous badger.

Tommy Brock's grin is a stroke of narrative brilliance on Potter's part. In the framing plot it is a sign of treacherous friendship. (All children learn to be wary of adult bonhomie, and Tommy is a dastardly example of it. He is the sort of person you do not take sweeties from.) This grin is repeatedly insisted upon, and in the main plot it is a danger signal. When we arrive at the inner plot, however, the grin mysteriously changes its nature. When Tommy Brock is sleeping in his boots in Mr Tod's bed, and Mr Tod is making elaborate arrangements to remove him, it is less clear who the hero is, and who the villain. Whose side is the child on? Tommy Brock is not really asleep: he is watching Mr Tod's activities through a half-open eye. And he is still grinning. (Every child who has pretended to be asleep when parents come round checking will have cause to grin with Tommy.) On the other hand, Tommy is a rabbitnapper, and deserves his comeuppance, so there is a thrilling moment when 'the grin was not quite so big'. All the same, as the intended vic-tim of a violent practical joke he enlists the reader's sympathy, so it is good that when he plans his reprisal he is 'grinning im-mensely'. By the skilful use of this single word and character trait, Potter transforms Tommy Brock from deceitful adult villain into naughty child.

The climax of Tommy Brock's childishness comes when he

has cunningly escaped the drenching that Mr Tod had plotted for him; 'He was quite dry himself and grinning; and he threw the cup of scalding tea all over Mr Tod.'

This is extremely funny: for the child reader, for the adult, for Beatrix Potter. It is the summit of anarchic naughtiness, and Potter's childness has a place for that. But it is also shocking, because these two powerful adults, Mr Tod and Tommy Brock, are quite evidently behaving as unruly children. Even the fussy householder, Mr Tod (a displaced parent-figure), has resorted to messy practical jokes to punish his adversary.

Moreover, there is an audience for these recreant misdoings. Underneath the house are hidden Benjamin and Peter, still on their mission to retrieve the little rabbits. They are a respectable pair, and suitably parental. But when they first arrive at the house, they move warily: there are dangerous 'adult' presences about. 'Peter and Benjamin flattened their noses against the window, and stared into the dusk.' At this point they are *children*, peeping into adult premises. The child reader is allied with them, as parents and as children, but placed in a superior position, at safe distance. When the contest between Tod and Brock descends through pranks to outright mayhem, Benjamin and Peter are in hiding, and they only hear what goes on, but the reader is the privileged audience, and sees it all.

The childness of this marvellous story has much to do with the power relationships between adult and child, the mystery of adulthood to children, and the strangely shifting balance of maturity between the child and adult as the child perceives it. This is made possible because the characters, as animals, move fluidly between childhood and maturity. Every character is a child's experiment with living. All this is achieved linguistically in the story, through the complex simplicity of Potter's prose, and it is also achieved narratively, by the device of the double plot and by the characterization this allows, which places every male character in the story (though not the females, Flopsy and Cottontail) at some point in the role of adult (either empowered or responsible) and at another of child (either inquisitive and mystified or very, very naughty).

I have previously argued that important experiences of childness are not limited to the children's book; that the separate category of 'children's literature' is in any case flexible (now you see it, now you don't); and that the presence or absence of a major child protagonist is a fallible guide to the depth and range of childness that a book may show. In the suggested list of questions designed to clarify the childness of a work, I also showed that some elements of childness are abstract, theoretical or symbolic, while others are linked to detailed sensitive observations of children or to vivid personal recall. I shall now try briefly to illustrate some of these points by taking two pairs of novels, in each case one by a major novelist for adults and one by a children's writer, and suggesting that the works in each pair have important features of childness in common.

CHARLES DICKENS, *OLIVER TWIST*; LEON GARFIELD, *SMITH*
If asked to pick a classic English novelist for whom childhood was a major theme and preoccupation, most readers would unhesitatingly choose Dickens. There are important depictions of childhood in *Oliver Twist, Nicholas Nickleby, The Old Curiosity Shop, Hard Times, Dombey and Son, David Copperfield*, and *Great Expectations*. Here, surely, we shall find a complex childness, and the last two of these novels certainly will not disappoint us. The others, on close examination, are likely to. Looking at Dickens's work as a whole, we find that the theoretical and symbolic elements of childhood are uppermost, and that children interested Dickens not as children but as images of pristine innocence and ideal human possibility, or as representative examples of personality distortion caused by adults, or more generally as a lens or measure by which adult practices can be socially and morally exposed.

The most important child images of distortion are Tom and Louisa Gradgrind and Bitzer in *Hard Times*, and Paul Dombey in *Dombey and Son*. All these children are denied a natural childhood and instead are subjected to massive educational pressure or to dogma-based behavioural training. (The ruinous effects of educational pressure have interested other novelists for adults, for example in Herman Hesse's *The Prodigy*.) These novels illustrate behaviouristic consequences following logically from this (often well-intentioned) mistreatment, and *virtually nothing else*. The particular consequence which Dickens vilifies is premature adulthood, a kind of youthful old age of the soul. We are likely to share Dickens's views of adult rights and wrongs in child development, and to see his power and importance as a crusader for enlightenment. However, as literary figures these children, *as children*, are virtually devoid of interest except for what they represent. They are essentially symbolic children, telling us not about themselves but about the adult world, and the childness with which they are invested is both generalized and narrow.

Oliver Twist, which is early Dickens, represents the other dominant strand in Dickensian childness, that of original innocence. Nothing, it seems, can corrupt his immaculate little heart. Indeed, the whole plot hinges on a theory of childhood innocence and goodness as realistic human possibility, and in a revealingly sexist way. The will of Oliver's natural father leaves half his property to Agnes Fleming's child (who is Oliver) with this stipulation: 'If it were a girl, it was to inherit the money unconditionally: but if a boy, only on the stipulation that in his minority he should never have stained his name with any public act of dishonour, meanness, cowardice or wrong.'

Although the grievous example of Monks is the direct cause for this in *Oliver Twist*, the gender-differentiated childness which it reveals is echoed elsewhere in Dickens. In *Hard Times* Tom Gradgrind is much worse corrupted than his sister, and the framing childhood possibilities are still more starkly contrasted in Bitzer and Cissy Jupe. In *Dombey and Son* Florence Dombey retains a warm human naturalness which is taught to death in Paul. Even the *Oliver Twist* adults show the same pattern, in the human compunction of Nancy set against the steel-hard evil of Bill Sikes. The girl in Dickens is more naturalistically good than the boy, but is also the admired subordinate in a sexually divided childness. Oliver Twist falls within this pattern. In satisfying his father's moral demands in spite of efforts to corrupt him, he symbolizes childhood as a possible state of natural innocence. He is a theorized virtuous child, narrowed to a representative significance, as in this passage where he muses on the likely death of Rose Maylie (Chapter 33) :

> Oliver turned homeward, thinking on the many kindnesses he had received from the young lady, and wishing that the time could come over again, that he might never cease showing her how grateful and attached he was. He had no cause for self-reproach on the score of neglect, or want of thought, for he had been devoted to her service; and yet a hundred little occasions rose up before him, on which he fancied he might have been more zealous, and more earnest, and wished he had been.

This passage precedes a miniature tutelary sermon for the adult reader, whose cause for regret is likely to exceed Oliver's. He is an example to us, and in being an example he loses all childness other than the theory of innocence. Dickens's narrative prose makes little effort to accommodate him as a real-life child.

The Artful Dodger, on the other hand, is an unusually cheerful instance of corruption. He is the happiest evidence in *Oliver Twist* that Dickens would one day write well about children: a cocky, humorous, streetwise survivor, prematurely adult in his criminal proficiency but not prematurely adult in his soul. Although his place in the narrative pattern is partly to reinforce Dickens's depiction of Fagin and his world (for which Oliver's naive judgements provide a magnifying lens) the Artful Dodger gets somewhat out of hand, and gathers shades of irresistible approval for his vigorous adaptability and good-humoured playing of the hand that life has dealt him. A different and more generous childness goes into his creation.

Leon Garfield's novels are widely praised for their Dickensian qualities, and he was a declared admirer of Dickens's work. And in fact a very similar pattern of strengths and weaknesses is evident in them. There is the vivid creation of a complete and stylized social world, based on the Hogarthian eighteenth century but decorated with a colourful and humorous grotesquerie which is essentially Dickensian in nature. There are ingenious and intricate plots and mysteries, often turning as in *Oliver Twist* on family feuds, intrigues and questions of inheritance. There is also a Dickensian addiction to stylistic exhibitionism which has won much praise and caused many schoolchildren to be taught that ingenious similes are the mark of a good writer, and as a rule there is a major child protagonist, none more prominent and central than Smith in *Smith*.

Smith is a twelve-year-old pickpocket in the streets of eighteenth-century London. Illiterate and poor, but intelligent and quick-witted, he plies his trade to fund his precarious toehold on security in the pub basement which he shares with his two older sisters. He is cheerful, streetwise, independent although capable of fierce affinities, and he knows his London.

Early in the story, Smith tracks an intended victim, an old man clearly unfamiliar with the city, and finally in a quiet courtyard brushes past him and relieves him of the papers in his pocket. Immediately afterwards, in hiding, he sees the old man murdered by two ruffians in search of these same papers.

"Oh! Oh! Oh my—" he murmured, gave a long sigh—and died.

His last sight on this earth had been of a small, wild and despairing face whose flooded eyes shone out of the shadows with all the dread and pity they were capable of.

(Smith was only twelve and, hangings apart, had seen no more than three men murdered in all his life.)

This is a cunning piece of writing, and is designed by a combination of sensational events and adroitly casual detail to achieve a double effect, and cast Smith in a double role which he will then maintain throughout the book. On the one hand there is Smith the pickpocket, the juvenile urban survivor, who lives in a violent society in which executions are a public enter-tainment, and who at twelve has already witnessed three mur-ders. On the other hand, there is Smith the boy, the appalled and helpless observer (very much like Oliver Twist, watching in horror as Mr Brownlow's pocket is picked at the bookseller's stall). This particular Smith, the boy, is not only shocked but capable of pity. Underneath his practised urchin criminality is a natural goodness and innocence, a natural generosity of spirit. Smith, that is to say, is an amalgam of Oliver Twist and the Artful Dodger. And just as Dickens in these two characters embodied in one text a double, even contradictory childness, so Garfield in the one character skilfully attempts to play it both ways, with a boy who represents childhood innocence while not being personally innocent. In both books, therefore, there are separate stereotypes of childness which are thinly conceived and func-tionally incompatible.

The illusion of consistency can only be sustained (by both Dickens and Garfield) by keeping an authorial distance and giv-ing play to irony and wit. For instance, when Smith escapes with his stolen document it is useless to him, because he cannot read it. Convinced nevertheless that it holds the key to better fortunes, he is desperate to learn to read. One night, himself now a fugitive from the assassins who know he has the docu-ment, he aids and befriends a blind magistrate, and in unlikely circumstances is adopted by his household. The magistrate's daughter teaches Smith to read, and quite soon there is a big step forward:

> He mastered the alphabet ... and, by the time of his meeting with the muffin-man, he could pronounce aloud such words as Miss Mansfield wrote on his slate.
>
> "M-y n-a-m-e i-s S-m-i-t-h ... th," he sputtered out with great difficulty, only understanding the sentiment as he heard the sounds he made.
>
> "Well done!" cried Miss Mansfield and Smith, though pleased to have pleased her, was mildly aggrieved to discover that so much effort had gone into saying aloud what was perfectly well known

to both of them all the time.

Thus might Dickens have written, and the reader might answer 'Oh no, he wasn't aggrieved, not even mildly.' A real-life Smith at this moment, making progress with a passionate ambition, would be overjoyed, pleased with himself as well as his teacher, and justifiably proud, feeling indeed that the Smithness of being Smith was advanced by the decoded sentence. He would *not* be aggrieved by its obviousness. This is an external joke on the author's part, an amused perception of incongruities between adult and child, which Smith is constructed to fit. Smith becomes an instrument for exposing Miss Mansfield's fallibility, in doing something which from the child's eye view is supposed to be silly. In this case it is not silly at all, but the incident is an example of Garfield's Dickensian use of Smith as an innocent angle of vision on the adult world.

If we ask, what in these novels are Dickens and Garfield really interested in, the answer is that they are interested in a London underworld and the bizarre individuality of its adult citizens; and they are interested in certain individuals and eccentric relationships (in Garfield's case the blind magistrate and his daughter) and they are especially interested in the phenomenon of treachery where loyalty should naturally be. But they are not, despite appearances, much interested in children, other than as narrative instruments. *Smith* is popular with child readers, as *Oliver Twist* traditionally has been, because it offers a simple child-role to ally with and a violent page-turning narrative that might appeal for its own sake to any reader; but not because either book offers a childness, a construction of childhood, which invites the child to explore himself through exploring the story.

Smith's most powerful scenes are set in Newgate Prison, where Smith, still in the livery he was given at Miss Mansfield's, lies accused of murdering the old man. Garfield's debt to Dickens is especially clear here, not least to Dickens's brilliant piece of reportage, 'A visit to Newgate', where in one of the wards he observes by the fireside 'a boy in livery', and in the condemned ward for those under sentence of death 'a handsome boy, not fourteen years old, and of singularly youthful appearance even for that age, who had been condemned for burglary'. The scene is powerful and vivid, but the boys serve mainly to illuminate its horrors; and so does Smith. Garfield's admiration for Dickens is a very mixed blessing for him as a children's writer.

D.H. LAWRENCE, *THE RAINBOW*
BERLIE DOHERTY, *WHITE PEAK FARM*

Few readers would nominate Lawrence among major writers with significant visions of childhood. *Sons and Lovers* is, among other more important things, a classic of adolescence, and a poem such as 'Piano' transforms nostalgia for lost childhood into something wholly unsentimental and profound, but in the main Lawrence is pre-eminently associated with adult relationships. Nevertheless Lawrence is a classic writer about childhood, who in relatively few specific passages articulates a deep and manifold childness. Its centrepiece in *The Rainbow* is Chapter 8, 'The Child'.

This chapter is largely about the infant Ursula Brangwen, the eldest daughter of Will and Anna Brangwen, whose marriage forms the second in the novel's three-generation structure. Ursula herself will be the central figure in the third generation. At this point she is still very young, just two or three, but her mother is already in the next stage of her unstoppable fecundity, and Ursula is taken over by her father, himself still a very young man. In 'The Child' Ursula is the recipient of her father's devoted love and attention, but she is also the innocent victim of the tensions between himself and Anna, and his emotional exile from her obsessive maternal self-fulfilment. So Ursula is both cosseted and mistreated, the puzzled captive of Will's mysterious and capricious fatherhood. She is successively loved and rejected. Since she in turn worships her father, his physical roughness and emotional brutalities have a profound effect upon her.

In this one chapter there is a sequence of representative

episodes, painful but unsensational in themselves, which cumulatively scar Ursula for life. She helps her father to set potatoes, but is over-eager and clumsy, and feels miserably unequal to her father's expectations. He says to her, 'You didn't help me much.' Another time she tramples across his seedbeds. 'If across the garden she saw the hedge had budded, and if she wanted these greeny-pink, tiny buds for bread-and-cheese, to play at tea-party with, over she went for them.' (The language of this sentence, with its sequence of impressions and impulses, the affectionate seriousness of 'to play at tea-party with', the movement of 'over she went', the inwardness of Lawrence's alliance with the girl, is a miniature gem of sympathetic childness.) Will is violently angry with her, for reasons that she cannot understand. On another occasion he swims and dives with her recklessly in the canal, and nearly drowns them both. When the fair comes, he takes her on the swingboats, and releases his frustrated energy in such huge swings that she is pale and sick.

Each episode is vivid and precise, acutely sensitive to the exact stage of Ursula's infancy and hence its effect on her development. Particulars merge into the general, as in this extraordinary, crucial paragraph after the seedbed incident:

> When she crawled out, after an hour or so, she went rather stiffly to play. She willed to forget. She cut off her childish soul from memory, so that the pain, and the insult should not be real. She asserted herself only. There was now nothing in the world but her own self. So very soon, she came to believe in the outward malevolence that was against her. And very early, she learned that even her adored father was part of this malevolence. And very early she learned to harden her soul in resistance and denial of all that was outside her, harden herself upon her own being.

In the third phase of the novel, the effects of these early experiences are visible in the adult Ursula, and the intricate psychological difficulty of her subsequent relationships. Naturally other and later experiences also harm her, but the early phase is fundamental and decisive. Lawrence is searchingly aware both of the separateness which cuts off infancy from the adult world (and hence the massive failures of comprehension that can happen between child and adult) and also of the continuity which causes infancy to resonate in the adult woman.

Ursula's own psychological story is part of a much larger one. *The Rainbow* is deeply embedded in social and cultural history. The first sentence of the novel starts, 'The Brangwens had lived for generations at the Marsh Farm . . . ' on the border between Derbyshire and Nottinghamshire. The men of the Brangwen family know the farm intimately—the land, the corn, the livestock—and they know and want nothing else. In autumn, as the seasonal cycle slows, 'the men sat by the fire and their brains were inert, as their blood flowed heavy with the accumulation from the living day.' The women, however, are different. 'They were aware of the lips and the mind of the world speaking and giving utterance, they heard the sound in the distance, and they strained to listen.' Ursula becomes the latest and—because the quickened pace of social history allows it—the most turbulent figure in the process of intellectual emancipation, with its consequent tussle between home and world, that has touched the consciousness of earlier Brangwen women.

Berlie Doherty's *White Peak Farm* is a linked sequence of ten short stories about the history of the Tanner family, which for generations has farmed White Peak Farm in the Derbyshire Peak District. The tales cover three generations, but are told by and concentrated in Jeannie, the third child of four in the youngest generation. At the close of the novel she is a university student, looking back over four years of her adolescence and early adulthood which have brought profound changes to her own life and that of her family. At the start she says of White Peak Farm, 'We've always lived here: my father's family has owned the farm for generations. He never wants to let it go.' And just as the Marsh Farm exists in a time-scale that precedes even the Brangwens, caught in an almost prehistoric stasis, so White Peak Farm includes a field which hides the remains of earlier, prehistoric settlements and nameless farmers of the land.

Yet Jeannie, like Ursula, is the product of a new intellectual emancipation. Modern social progress means that she can leave the farm and go to Oxford, to the wide world of the mind and the geographical mobility of present-day life. She is not the only one to leave. Her older brother Martin is a gifted artist as well as a good farmer, and he goes away to art school: emancipation is not the privilege or ambition of girls only. But one day Martin will return to farm his inheritance. Jeannie will return, as the last sentence makes clear, but only as a visitor.

Two generations before Jeannie, her grandmother faced equivalent choices, and she is the subject of the first, intensely moving and important story. ('Gran' in *White Peak Farm* is one of the best pieces of writing I know in the whole of modern children's literature. Its qualities of childness are profound. As a picture of inter-generational relationships, of self in family, of growth and individuality and discovery of selfhood, of making a future, it has things to say that matter to every child. There is not a child of real importance in it, unless you count adolescents; but the story is full to bursting with significant *youth*, both past and present.) Gran too went to Oxford, a great thing in her day, but had to return to the village for good after a year, to care for her sick mother. Like the Brangwen women's, her life is one of unused possibilities: a frame of reference for modern youth, especially for girls.

Life at White Peak Farm is not easy, because the father, John Tanner, is a closed, moody and censorious man, estranged and isolated from his family by damaged pride, turned inward on the farm as his whole world, emotionally rough and insensitive to his wife and children, indifferent to daughters. Socially, intellectually, in his horizons, he has things in common with the Brangwen men, good things as well as bad. The good things are harder to see, and a trite urban humanism would dismiss them altogether, but Lawrence does not, and nor does Doherty. But parents like Tanner are hard for children to live with, whether they are infants like Ursula, or adolescents like Jeannie. The parallel with Will Brangwen is evident in the opening of 'The Hired Hand':

We were a house of secrets. We all of us kept our thoughts and our hopes to ourselves. Whether it's the way of country people, who count long hours of solitude as a way of life, I don't know. Maybe it was the effect my father had on us; his way of belittling our individuality.

This is a muted version of Ursula's ordeal in infancy, but essentially the cause and consequence are the same.

Doherty's world is a kinder, more forgiving one than Lawrence's, but offers no soft options. *White Peak Farm*, which is very short and very approachable, is the equivalent of *The Rainbow* for children, touching on similar themes and key experiences. Its childness rests in its authentic portrait of growth, the experiences which teach and harden us (because adolescent Jeannie, like infant Ursula, *is* hardened); of time as children experience it, first standing still, then racing; of tensions in the family and generations; of watching your elders' crises, only to find yourself trapped by them in your turn. Except for Marion, the youngest daughter, all the characters are adults and adolescents, and Jeannie as one of them has a believably articulate voice. But the experiences are known to much younger children, and the small scale of the book invites them in. Children's fiction can have young children without significant childness, but it can also have, as here, a masterpiece of childness without young children.

RE-IMAGINING CHILDNESS: ROBERT WESTALL
THE MACHINE-GUNNERS & YAXLEY'S CAT

I argued earlier that it is incumbent on present-day children's writers to re-imagine childness. Childhood has changed in recent years. Its duration, sophistication, and relationship to adulthood are not what they were. In particular, the balance of power between child and parent has changed, and with it the basis on which good family relationships are built. If the neo-children of our times are to take children's literature seriously, as entertainment which can rival Stephen King or video games, they must find in it reflections of the childness they experience

110

directly. Because children are literate in the media and sophisticated in their 'reading' of media fictions, they can adapt to alternative conventions of childhood, provided they are not expected to regard images of yesterday's childness as their own contemporaries. Children's literature must do its best—as Joan Aiken said of teenage literature—to include images of the present.

To illustrate these points, we can take as examples two novels by Robert Westall. Both of them have as a central protagonist a boy of twelve or thirteen, and both of them are about guns.

The Machine-Gunners was Westall's first published book, and is still his best-known. Set in North Shields and Tynemouth ('Garmouth' in the book) during the blitz on Tyneside in the Second World War, the book is in many respects autobiographical. Westall wrote it for his son, then aged twelve, 'to show him how life had been for me at twelve'. Although the central incident was based on a wartime exploit by Dutch teenagers, in the Zuyder Zee, the background and characters are directly drawn from the author's memory. The dedication, for example, is explicit : 'To my mother and father who *were* the mother and father of the book.' Unconscious revisionism will certainly be at work. For example, Stan Liddell, the teacher and Home Guard Officer who is a rare example of intelligent adult officialdom in the story, is based on Westall's much-loved English teacher, and stands a little apart as an idealized figure of heroic common sense. But as far as it lay in Westall's power (which was considerable) the book is a feat of authentic memory. The children are as children were.

Twelve-year-old boys in wartime Garmouth collect souvenirs of war—pieces of shrapnel and other trophies of the blitz. Early in the story Chas McGill, aged twelve, finds the greatest of all souvenirs. He discovers a crashed German aircraft which the authorities have not found, with the decomposing body of the German pilot still inside it. With the help of his friends, Chas removes a machine-gun and ammunition from the plane, and bears them away in secret concealed in a Guy-cart. Eventually Chas and his friends laboriously construct their own machine-gun emplacement, in the grounds of a bombed house where one of the group has lived. Their further complicating triumph is to capture a German airman, Rudi, who has parachuted from a crashing enemy plane. Confined in their secret machine-gun nest, Rudi gradually befriends the children (five boys and a girl) and it is partly through his eyes that we get a reliable external view of them.

Many of the questions about childness which I posed in the last chapter can be asked productively of *The Machine-Gunners*. Notable among them might be 'How old are the children?' We know their official ages: they are twelve or thirteen, in the third form at the grammar school. These children at that age collect war souvenirs as they might collect stamps. At first the machine-gun and its hiding-places are a game, a thrilling enterprise of imitative heroics which is also an act of separation and defiance aimed at the repressive world of adults. As time goes on, and in particular as they realize the harm done by adults to two of their number, the rebellious enterprise becomes more serious, a fiercely loyal child conspiracy against the grown-ups. The machine-gun nest becomes their fortress.

> So they brought the gun out of its wrapping, and laid Granda's Union Jack on it, and everyone put their hands on the gun and swore to look after Nicky. In the swearing, Fortress Caparetto became more than a game; it became a nation. And the Germans ceased to be the only enemies. All the adults were a kind of enemy now . . .

The game turns deadly earnest, and as its consequences take hold, the children both are and are not children, as Rudi comes to appreciate. There is a problem with the machine-gun, and only Rudi can mend it:

> It would be wrong to give children back a gun like that. Because they *were* still children. But somehow, he couldn't insult them by *saying* that. Because, in another way, they were no longer children.

Just as in William Golding's *Lord of the Flies* the children's barbarity is always contextualized by the reader's knowledge that adult warfare caused the children's plight in the first place (and they are rescued by a cruiser), so the children's war-game in *The Machine-Gunners* is contextualized by the larger war-game being played around them. If the children gain an odd maturity in their secret mission, there are childish adults in the world they are defying, typified by the eccentric Free Polish forces whom the kids mistake for Germans in the invasion scare which brings the story to a climax. There is a batty logic in the children's game. But however serious and ultimately catastrophic, it is still in the end a game, played by young children as an appalling prank. The adults, however flawed themselves, hold ultimate power and authority which is never questioned. And the children are innocents, pre-sexual and immature: there is never a sexual dimension to Audrey Parton's presence in their ranks. Their exploits are both comic and terrible, and end in dangerous, almost lethal farce. Between them and the grown-ups, a wide division gapes.

Yaxley's Cat is utterly different. This is the story of two children, Tim aged thirteen and his sister Jane, a year or so younger, who persuade their mother to rent a tumbledown holiday cottage which they find by chance in Norfolk. Their mother, whose holiday is a temporary flight from her rich, super-efficient, morale-sapping husband, agrees. In doing so she cedes power to the children. The story is told entirely from the mother's point of view; it is adult-centred. But this particular adult is controlled by two formidable children—worldly, knowing, shrewd and capable.

This is just as well. The cottage they have chanced on was the home of a dead 'cunning man', or witch, and is situated on the edge of a remote, isolated, inbred village peopled by hostile rustics and dominated by violent pre-Christian superstition. When Rose, the mother, is herself identified by these people as a witch, the family become the hapless victims of a murderous attack.

At any rate the mother is hapless. Not so the children. Tim

has a gun, a long black air-pistol.

'Tim, for heaven's sake, what good is an *air-pistol*?'
'It's a .22. It can go through a plank of wood at fifty yards. Dad and I tried it, down Bunty's pit. It's Yugoslav — '
'Tim, you wouldn't shoot . . . '
'Bloody would,' he said, taking a small shiny pellet from the box that was bulging his pyjama pocket and putting it carefully into the barrel. He closed the air-pistol with a reassuring click.

And he bloody does. When one of the rustics hits his mother, Tim blows a hole in his hand that you can see the light through. Until help arrives at the end of this exciting (and quite believable) story, Tim and Jane are competent, cool citizens of the perilous world. Their mother emphatically is not. She can only look on appalled as they protect her—calmly, with amusement, with condescending love.

Tim's first field action is against Jack Sydenham, the local shopkeeper, who makes passes at his mother on a remote footpath. Tim blows his hat off as a warning. Sydenham tries adult bluster, threatening Tim with the police.

'Please do,' said Timothy. 'Then I can tell them how you were manhandling my mother. Common assault. If not indecent assault, eh, Jane? And three witnesses against one. You haven't got a prayer, chum.'

This is a different world of childhood from that of *The Machine-Gunners*. The cool assurance, the assumption of equality (if not superiority) with adults, the sexual knowingness, the sheer street cred of youth, would be unthinkable in wartime Garmouth. Tim is not just one year older than Chas McGill. He is also fifty years younger. This is the 1990s against the 1940s, and in mind and body Tim is several years ahead of Chas, as Jane is of Audrey.

Westall does not quite know what to make of his creation. Part of him, through Rose, is appalled by modern childhood.

She remembered an army colonel talking on the radio once. Young men make the best soldiers, he had said. Eighteen-year-olds, even sixteen-year-olds, make the best killers. They have no imagination; they do not understand what it is to inflict or suffer pain and death. How about thirteen-year-olds? she thought wildly. She had read of thirteen-year-olds committing murder. In America even ten- or eleven-year-olds. With guns. It was all a video game to them, at that age.

We have all heard of that by now. A part of Westall shares his character's horror, and diagnoses its origins in the media.

All the movies had come home to Tim. *Dirty Harry, Lethal Weapon II, Full Metal Jacket, Rambo, The Exterminator.* Barred from the cinema, forbidden them at home, Tim had watched them all at friends' houses. Over and over. They had started their GCSE in killing a year early . . .

But another part of Westall is drawn to admiration for the boy's proficiency and competence, his confident mastery of his world, and recognizes something in it which cannot be blamed on videos, but lies in the dizzying social evolution of the modern child.

Children enjoy *The Machine-Gunners* as an exciting historical novel. But in *Yaxley's Cat*, I suspect, they find an image of themselves, as they are or wish to be and can be. For better or worse, something has happened to childhood, and Westall has observed it. With great honesty and courage, in the years that separate *The Machine-Gunners* from *Yaxley's Cat,* he has re-imagined childness.

7

'Only the young have such moments'

The second key word of this study is 'youth' (see pages 60-1). It forms the central term in this chapter. 'Youth' is a simpler and more familiar term than 'childness', but is equally essential to my argument. 'Childness' directs attention chiefly to the distinctive features of childhood, as we first of all live it, then remember and negotiate with and provide for it. 'Youth' focuses our minds on continuities which lengthen and blur the boundary between childhood and adult life. Two groups of texts are chosen here to exemplify different aspects of a 'literature of youth'.

The first group of stories shows how a commonplace but important childhood event can be treated at different levels of complexity. Catherine Storr's *Robin* is written about a small child for child readers of Robin's age; at the other extreme Graham Swift's 'Learning to Swim' is written about the same childhood event but for adults (not even young adults), assuming that its interest and significance have no time limit.

The second group of texts again share a particular event, this time showing how the event retains its powers of epiphany into the twenties, and therefore into what we call 'adult life'. 'Youth' is a long suspension bridge between childhood and adulthood, and these stories demonstrate its length and psychological importance in terms not only of texts and potential reading events but of actual lived experience.

Both events could be matched in life and literature by many others, including many which carry much greater psychological complexity. Some of the texts discussed would not normally be considered 'children's literature' as earlier defined, but all of them fall within a 'literature of youth'.

*

In H.G. Wells's short story 'The Door in the Wall' the leading character, Lionel Wallace, undergoes a seemingly magical experience as a five-year-old boy. Lionel is a lonely child—motherless, brotherless, sisterless, the offspring of an aloof but ambitious father with high expectations for his future. Precocious and mature for his age, Lionel wanders away from home and the care of his nursery governess into the streets of London. He comes to a green door in a white wall, and feels a strong desire to go through it, though at the same time he is sure it would be wrong or unwise to do so. The narrator reports: 'He insisted upon it as a curious thing that he knew from the very beginning—unless memory has played him the queerest trick—that the door was unfastened, and that he could go in as he chose.'

Go in he does, and slams the door behind him. 'And so, in a trice, he came into the garden that has haunted all his life.' The enchanted garden which he finds behind the green door is a uniquely happy place. There he finds docile and friendly panthers, an older girl to befriend and guide him, playmates to relieve his loneliness. With these new friends he plays delightful games which afterwards he struggles unavailingly to remember. 'In the instant of coming into [the garden] one was exquisitely glad—as only in rare moments, and when one is young and joyful one can be glad in this world. And everything was beautiful there . . . '

Presently he is summoned away from the childhood idyll by a sombre woman who shows him the pages of a picture book containing the story of his life up to that day, until the moment of his entry to the garden. But when the next page turns, it does not show him the garden he has found. Instead the picture—which like all the earlier ones is also reality—returns him to grey London streets, and exile from the paradise he has stumbled upon. And afterwards: 'as a child, I spent long hours trying, even with tears, to recall the form of that happiness. I wanted to *play it all over again*—in my nursery—by myself [my italics].'

The strangest part of the story is that from time to time for the rest of his life and throughout a successful adult political career Lionel again sees the green door in the white wall—always briefly and without warning—and has chances to re-enter it. Each time he feels the urge to go through but refuses the opportunity. The apparition of the door as Wells recounts it seems to occur at moments of transition and development in Lionel's life: when he is travelling to Oxford to take a scholarship exam, when he is on the way to visit a lover who doubts him, when his father is dying, when his political advancement is at stake. The attractions of the doorway to a lost childhood, and the attractions of adult love and duty and success cause in him 'a double and divergent movement of my will'. Finally he is killed when he goes through a small door in the boarding of an excavation for extension of the London Underground, and falls into a deep pit. Was it tragic accident, or ultimate re-entry to what only he could see?

In the ambivalences of this remarkable story we find a classic fictive statement of the 'double and divergent' movement of the will which lies at the heart of childhood, and of the imaginative experiences that children's literature can offer to reflect, support and clarify it. In Lionel Wallace's story, child-being is set against child-becoming. Both are necessary. In his case child-being is impoverished by his solitude, his mother's death, his father's coldness, his own precocity. The enchanted garden idyllically supplies what life does not. Because there is a hole in his childhood, the epiphany of child-being represented by the garden becomes a too-important need in later life, especially when re-traced upon the mind through the blanks and uncertainties of memory. If such experiences of fulfilled companionship and play are missing or too rare in childhood, the adult's life is likely to be compromised by hopeless efforts to recover them. In one way or another, literally or metaphorically, the effort can be fatal. Child-being is very important, and reflections of child-being in story are important also. We need our Blytons and our Dahls, just as slightly later we need Sweet Valley High.

But as Lionel's refusals of the door suggest, child-becoming is equally or more important, as indeed in a fulfilled life is adult-becoming also. 'All children, except one, grow up.' And so we should. Geoffrey Trease, who has never deviated from the sane view that childhood exists to be left behind, said in a television programme about his work: 'My attitude has always been, "Never mind the childish world. Come on and join the adult. It is terrible in places, but it's also fun, and you've got to come anyhow."' We may not agree wholly with this. My argument has been that it is impossible not to 'mind' the world of our childhood, because it is always part of us. And 'childish' is in any case a misconceived description of it. But the general force and rightness of Trease's urging is beyond dispute. Lionel Wallace in Wells's story is unable to reconcile the 'double and divergent' movements of his will, the need to be and also to become.

A well-lived and properly cared-for childhood will enable children to live happily with the doubleness and reconcile the contradictory needs. A satisfying experience of literature and story will minister to the contradictions and supply images of this doubleness, which is endemic to human growth. This is why I have argued that we need to reawaken the word 'youth' in our thinking about children's reading. We need the term 'literature of youth' to run simultaneously with 'children's literature' in our language, each term in critical dialogue with the other just as the experiences they represent are in constant dialogue within the reader.

We need to remember, always, that youth can be very long, extending into the early stages of adult life. And we need to remember that although it is long, and a continuum, it is also marked by significant moments, for which we can properly use the Joycean term 'epiphanies'. Such moments vary in their nature. Some (like Lionel Wallace's idyll in the enchanted garden) are encapsulations of total childhood, fusions of actual or desired experience in single, unforgettable events. Others are times and moments when we feel our lives on the turn—irreversible movements forward into adult life, achievements of independence, confidence and control, proofs of self-value and of value in the eyes of others. Epiphanies such as these can be public and social, or private and secret. They can be lastingly remembered and permanently strengthening, or (a hard category, this) devoid of further significance once the moment of immediate euphoria has passed. In childhood and youth we can understand them better if we find them authentically reflected in story, and they can image for us the unspoken goals and values of the culture we inhabit.

If my argument has been followed thus far, it will be clear that I think such epiphanies are essential to effective growth, and that any society which does not have a coherent set of accepted goals and values, together with images by which we and our children can define them, is at risk. It risks converting rebellion, which is natural and necessary, into severance, which is not. If the tacit underlying continuity is broken, a youth culture may opt for epicurean nihilism instead. Literature is a powerful means by which such images are articulated to the young, but the literature cannot always be easy, or reached by young readers without help. Parents and teachers are there to represent the goals and values of a culture (which they will do anyway, whether they intend to or not) and it is also their job to mediate the complex images of story.

Children need all this. If the culture is exposed as incoherent and confused, children will detect it, no matter what hypocrisies or concealments adults may resort to. If the images and stories are not there, or the criteria of worth and value are denied, the youth culture will invent its own. And if we do not like what they invent, we have only ourselves to blame. Literature may seem a small and marginal part of many people's lives, but image and story, with all the values—good and bad—that they imply, are not marginal at all.

I shall conclude this study, therefore, with two examples of representative significant subjects in a 'literature of youth'.

Both subjects and texts are intended only as examples. The central events are simple and traditional, and few of the texts are recent. Intentionally, they are taken from times when texts about childhood were 'assured of certain certainties', in ways that for the moment we have lost. *The Voyage of the 'Frog'*, and other popular books by Gary Paulsen, show that traditional subjects still have life, but to many readers they will seem old-fashioned.

I choose them in order to suggest a question. What have we put in their place? If such themes, events and texts are obsolete—if they no longer give children powerful vicarious images of initiation into positive adulthood, and shared terms of reference by which they can evaluate their growth—then what are the themes, events and texts that have replaced them? These books imagine childhood and youth in ways that formed a common currency with readers in countless important reading events. All embody elements of childness as I depicted its concerns in Chapter 5. They focus upon moments of significant transition in the processes of growth. If these transitions are now obsolete, what are their equivalents in contemporary life and story? There is something wrong if this is a question that we cannot answer confidently.

Most of the examples concern boys. This is a pragmatic response to the facts of late twentieth-century life. Girls have parallel and equivalent needs for positive experience in both life and story, but girls at the time of writing seem to be making a better job of growing up than boys are. On the whole it is not girls who carry knives, commit assaults, steal cars and crash them. Boys rather than girls resort to negative demonstrations of self-worth. Boys rather than girls currently feel surplus to society's requirements.

The following discussion therefore concerns fictions of transition, engaging with issues of worth, self-proof and adult membership, deriving mainly from an earlier, less contentious time. Whether the positives were socially desirable is not the point. The point is that they were *perceived* as positive, and there to be believed in.

The two topics I have chosen are learning to swim and to dive, and sailing a boat, either as lone sailor or on first command, in dangerous waters.

Catherine Storr's story *Robin* is intended for young children of perhaps seven or eight. Robin is the youngest of three children, with all the disadvantages that this involves. His great need is to outdistance his brother and sister at least in one area of their lives. When he finds a remarkable shell on the beach near their seaside home, Robin divines its name (as opposed to naming it): it is called the Freedom of the Seas. The shell has magical powers, and its gift to Robin is his very own freedom of the seas: intuitive understanding of water, and sea-creatures, and the storms of the sea. When he finds the shell Robin is just about to start learning to swim. After his first school swimming lesson he announces to his disbelieving family that he can swim already. Nobody can swim after just one lesson, his sister says. But the next visit to the beach proves that indeed he can. *Robin* is a story of sea-magic, and swimming is only a part of it. Nevertheless in a psychologically true and important way Robin's speed of learning and new-found proficiency give him the exhilaration of self-furtherance and a change of status in his family. With this new skill, and the excitement of its first display, his life moves on. He will never be 'the youngest' in the same way again.

For readers a year or two older, Philippa Pearce's story 'Return to Air' enacts the same experience with diving. The girl in her story (called 'Sausage') is already a strong swimmer, but she cannot see without her glasses and so has never learned to dive. Persuaded to learn duck-diving instead, she is told by her swimming instructor to dive after a brick which he will throw into the pond where they swim. Down she goes into the murky depths of the pond, and seizes what she takes to be the brick. Now she must swim up with her burden and resurface. At this point the story is one of fear: fear of the sightless depths, of having lost direction, of being cut off from life-replenishing air. Then at last she breaks surface, and finds that her trophy is not the brick at all but an old tin that has lain for years on the pond bottom, heavy with mud. Afterwards she learns to duck-dive well, but that first experience is the epiphany, the unique and unforgettable one, the triumph over fear and challenge in the watery dark. The last paragraph of the story articulates the childness of the story, and the experience it opens up for child readers:

I've cleaned the tin up and I keep it on the mantelpiece at home with my coin collection in it. I had to duck-dive later for another brick, and I got it all right, without being frightened at all; but it didn't seem to matter as much as coming up with the tin. I shall keep the tin as long as I live, and I might easily live to be a hundred.

Only the first time matters. Life cruelly transforms epiphany into commonplace, achievement into mere performance. But the first time is unforgettable.

Doris Lessing's 'Through the Tunnel' is another story of ordeal by diving, but more psychologically intricate and inexplicit. An eleven-year-old boy, an only child on a seaside holiday abroad with his widowed mother, observes some local boys swimming off rocks. Needing companionship, he tries to join them. They are older than he is, and though they are friendly, his would-be-comic overtures embarrass them and they go away. Before they do, however, he has observed a feat of underwater swimming that they perform, and on investigating he finds that they swim the length of a submarine tunnel from one side of the rocks to the other. The boy is an accomplished swimmer, but this ferocious challenge to the lungs and body obsesses him. Training himself by ever more rigorous demands on his breathing, he finally accomplishes the dive and swim in a self-imposed ordeal of private danger. The dive becomes an arbitrary and symbolic test (in physical but also other, more important senses)of his fitness. Lessing calls it 'the adventure that was so necessary to him'. Finally, worn out by his secret triumph, he tells his mother at lunch that he can stay   under water 'for two minutes—three minutes at least.' 'It came bursting out of him.' Calm but concerned, his mother tells him not to overdo it. 'She was ready for a battle of wills, but he gave in at once. It was no longer of the least importance to go to the bay.'

The childness embodied in the boy's maturational experience is meaningful and important to young readers, but the narrative frame is detached, laconic, poised with great skill between observation and empathy, matching the implied gap in the boy's mind between action and retrospect, the doing of a thing and the thing done. The story is not obscure, and has manifest significance for young readers, but it will only be accessible unaided to a minority of teenagers.

The sophistication is more pronounced still in Graham Swift's story, 'Learning to Swim'. This story concerns a married couple with a six-year-old son, Paul. The couple are badly matched. Mr Singleton, an engineer, is a powerful swimmer who won prizes in his youth. Largely indifferent to sexuality, pleasure and all emotion, whether of fear or delight, he has used first swimming and later engineering as a pretext for disengagement from the rest of life. Mrs Singleton, sensually generous but unwanted and unfulfilled, turns instead towards her son. Paul is the subject of contest between them. Now that he is six, Mr Singleton can teach him to swim, thereby acquiring a new substitute for life's complexities. But Paul is afraid of the water, humiliated by his incapacity, and humiliated also by his father's ambitious coaching and his mother's engulfing protective love.

At the end a story which has seemed to be about the parents proves to be really about Paul. Trapped one day at a swimming lesson between his father's and mother's exactions, he suddenly learns to swim—not only with his body, but his mind. 'But then, perhaps he was not afraid of his mother nor his father, nor the water, but of something else.' Simultaneously with this thought, his body gains freedom of the water:

'Towards me ! Towards me!' said his father suddenly. But he kicked and struck, half in panic, half in pride, away from his father, away from the shore, away, in this strange new element that seemed all his own.

Youngest of all the children in these stories, Paul is the subject of the subtlest literary treatment. By learning to swim he gains independence, gains himself, defeats his fear. But will it be the true independence of confident life to which all youth should be moving, or will it be a vacuum-sealed proficiency of solitary excellence to replicate his father's? It feels like the first, and suggests the exhilaration of true release, but the ambiguity is still left unresolved.

With the same symbolic action at their centre, all these stories explore the momentous transitional episodes of youth, and show their beginnings in early childhood. Properly introduced by a competent adult reader, Graham Swift's story for adults can illuminate for teenagers their own processes of growth by showing them erupting in a six-year-old. But that will be all the easier if they read stories such as *Robin* earlier. A 'literature of youth' is comprehensive indeed.

The second group of stories are about those who go down to the sea in ships, and do business in great waters. Danger at sea is common to them all, and so is the experience for a boy or a young man of solo voyaging or first command. The youngest of these captains is fourteen; the oldest in his early twenties. Youth and the passage to adulthood do not end with the teenage years.

Jill Paton Walsh's *The Dolphin Crossing*, written early in her career, is the odd one out within the group of texts, being the only book about war, the only one to have a strongly national, political dimension. A historical novel, although the history is modern, it is a story of the Dunkirk evacuation in 1940. Famously, the British Expeditionary Force was taken off the Dunkirk beaches by the 'little ships'—a strange assortment of boats and sailors from English ports. Seventeen-year-old John Aston, a merchant captain's son, takes the family boat and with his friend Pat crosses the Channel and performs heroic deeds in the heat and horror of war. When they return safely with some of those they have rescued, Pat—who is no sailor—takes the boat to sea again in an act of quixotic bravery and is lost, leaving John with the accumulated truths, deeds and anguish of all they have done.

The book is carefully researched, historically accurate, and skilfully told. It is a documentary novel, and a partisan one. The author's sense of alliance and common cause with her protagonists is sometimes openly declared. At one point John is angered by the machine-gun attacks of German planes on helpless soldiers. 'Then', the narrator tells us, 'he realized that *our own* pilots [my italics] would do the same, if the positions of the two armies were reversed.'

In some ways, then, this is a novel which gives primacy to behaviour and events over inward experience and personal psychology. John Aston is by turns happy, and sad, and frightened, and angry, and resolute; overall, he is very brave. The characterization is not stinted or oversimplified, yet it is finally unconvincing. The reason for this is the imaginative absence of that core experience which would surely have been there for a John Aston: the irreversible transformative endurance of reality, the quickening romance of selfhood which even the darkest of such episodes brings with it in youth, the traumatic sacrifice of left-over childhood, the crossing of a personal shadow line into maturity. The scale and nature of John's personal convulsion, as it would certainly have been, is subdued by the public reality of war. John is a very good, decisive, uncompromising captain who triumphantly survives the test of first command. The external starknesses of war should not obscure imaginatively the personal evolution it is sure to bring.

Gary Paulsen's novel *The Voyage of the 'Frog'* shows the life still active in this theme. The fourteen-year-old protagonist, David Alspeth, has been asked by his dying sailor-uncle to scatter his ashes on the open ocean, out of sight of land. His uncle's little sailing-boat, the *Frog*, is now David's own. Sailing alone off California, he duly performs the task for someone he loved, and whose sailing apprentice he has been. Then he is caught in a storm, carried far out to sea with few supplies, and in a life-changing ordeal of small-boat survival he experiences the wonders and the dangers of the sea. At one point, almost run down and yet unsighted by a tanker, he undergoes a crisis of hatred, against his parents and his dead uncle, against the elements, against himself. 'And in the end, in the steaming little pit of hatred and poison, he found himself, he found the David he needed.'

This is a story of youth, of growth, of self-discovery, of maturation through solitary captaincy. It seems to me a convincing and distinguished story. What sets it in the exemplary tradition I am tracing is that it is also about epiphanies, about moments of

transformative exhilaration and joy. As he gains control of himself and his ship, the two become one in a moment of—so to
speak—whole-body vision, an epiphany indeed. He says to the
boat, 'I guess we should reef sail if the wind is going to keep
getting stronger.'

> And he meant we—he could no longer draw a line where he
> ended and the *Frog* began. He looked down at his bare feet,
> planted firmly on the floor of the cockpit, the vibration, the hum,
> the life of the *Frog* coming up through them into his legs, and he
> knew it would be we from now on. They were together, a thing of
> the sea and the wind and man all joined in a single dance.
> To sail.
> To turn the force of the wind and sea, the force of the earth and
> a person, into a dance across the water.

And at the end, when David has accepted help from a trawler
but refused to abandon his boat, the story rightly closes on the
quiet note of mature practicality to which epiphanies must give
way: 'He had some sailing to do.'

'Children's literature' and 'literature of youth' co-exist at their
most impressive in Arthur Ransome's classic story *We Didn't
Mean to Go to Sea*. In this book the four Walker children, the
'Swallows' of *Swallows and Amazons* and several later books, find
that the adventurous but sheltered play of earlier times has
suddenly been overtaken by life-and-death reality. Their student
friend Jim Brading's boat, the *Goblin*, has dragged its anchor in
fog while Jim is ashore, and despite a promise to their mother
not to go outside Harwich harbour they find themselves in the
North Sea in foul weather, and at night. The voyage they make
to Flushing is a rite of passage for them all, but especially for
John, the eldest, the erstwhile skipper of the *Swallow*, who for
this one night finds himself captain of the *Goblin*, with all his
childhood play and learning put to the severest possible test.

It is impossible to summarize all that the children learn from
the alarms and emergencies of their traumatic night, such as
Susan's discovery that sometimes the letter of a promise must be

broken so that the spirit of it can be kept. Nothing about the journey is romanticized, heroicized, or made unrealistically easy, and the practicalities of survival are always at the forefront of the story. But the children all do well, and John in his first command does especially well. His own epiphany, his joyous intuition and acceptance of maturity, comes when all the others are asleep, and he is sailing the boat alone:

> He had done his very best. And anyhow, here, at night, far out in the North Sea, what could he do other than what he was doing? If anybody could have seen his face in the faint glimmer from the compass window, he would have seen that there was a grin on it. John was alone in the dark with his ship, and everybody else was asleep. He, for that night, was the Master of the *Goblin*, and even the lurches of the cockpit beneath him as the *Goblin* rushed through the dark filled him with a serious kind of joy. He and the *Goblin* together. On and on. On and on. Years and years hence, when he was grown up, he would have a ship of his own and sail her out into wider seas than this. But he would always and always remember this night when for the first time ship and crew were in his charge, his alone.

This is great writing for children. 'For children' is a definition of its greatness, not a reductive qualification of it. In the terms I have used in this study, we can see the residual and unfinished childness of John's being: the grin, the satisfied sense of having earned adult praise, the consummation of child-being. But there is also youth, and child-becoming: the visionary sense (like David Alspeth's) of oneness with the ship, the acceptance of captaincy and with it the responsibility it brings, the 'serious kind of joy'. And mediated by the omniscient narrator, there is the realization that this moment of time is enormously significant, always to be remembered. Ransome's key phrasing is sometimes childly: 'years and years', 'always and always'. But these same phrases are imbued with a wholly adult celebratory passion for the solemn wonder of the human experience he is recording. The writing is filled with a love of life, because life affords such transcendent moments.

This passage in *We Didn't Mean to Go to Sea* is pivotal for the book, but arguably also for the entire twelve-volume series, a collective work of incomparable low-key greatness which is all about the role of play, and of reading as play, in making such rites of passage achievable in life and in story for thousands of John Walkers. Ransome, as we noted earlier, professedly wrote to please himself. In *We Didn't Mean to Go to Sea* there is no mistaking the integrity of imaginative passion which underlies the practical story, and hence no problem in believing him.

John Masefield's *The Bird of Dawning* is not conventionally children's literature as earlier defined, but it is certainly literature of youth. The hero of this novel is one 'Cruiser' Trewsbury. 'Cruiser' is twenty-one, and second mate on the China clipper *Blackgauntlet*, a contender in the celebrated 'tea race'. When *Blackgauntlet* is rammed by a steamer and sunk, Cruiser finds himself with his own first command—a pitifully supplied ship's boat, filled with a motley crew of survivors and afloat in the ocean vastness. In the final romantic and compelling episode of the story, they find another China clipper, *Bird of Dawning*, abandoned for no evident reason. (On the orders of a mad captain, it later transpires.) They board her, and sail her to victory in the tea race.

Much could be said about this excellent story, positioned as it is on the margins of children's literature, but I wish here simply to point out the strong resemblances between Cruiser Trewsbury and John Walker. Cruiser is a well-qualified, well-educated, professional ship's officer, but for him too this is a first command, and for him too there is a pattern of stresses and exhilarations and tests, and a sense of irreversible forward movement to maturity. He, too, at twenty-one, experiences the ostensibly irrational but nonetheless profound and true exultancy which Paulsen and Ransome register, and which—however incongruous its presence might seem in the horrors of Dunkirk—I still find implausibly absent in *The Dolphin Crossing*. Here is Cruiser, in extreme danger, in a tiny boat on the great ocean:

There was no life in sight in all that beauty, save theirs, as they drove on ...To Cruiser steering there came from that fact an exaltation that he was the master of this vastness, that his will and imagination would bring this little frail, patched, leaking, spotted scarecrow of a crowded ship's boat, safe across the pathless sea to a haven. He looked at the sun and he looked at the sea, and said to them within his heart: 'Perhaps I'll do you yet.'

Emancipated from orthodox categorical boundaries by the term 'literature of youth', we are led on a continuum of experience and insight to fictions which rank with the greatest of all. The narrator of Joseph Conrad's 'Youth' is Marlow, his narrator-within-the-novel for several major works, including *Lord Jim*. In 'Youth' Marlow at forty-two is telling a story about himself at twenty. A little junior to Trewsbury at the same period of history, Marlow has been third officer on a clipper and has now signed on as second mate of the *Judea*, a dilapidated barque bound with a cargo of coal to Bangkok. After numerous mishaps this old ship at last reaches the Indian Ocean, but there her cargo catches fire and she is lost. So Marlow too achieves his first command, and for him too it is a ship's boat. In 'Youth' the consummation of inner romance which rivals Cruiser's triumph in the tea race is a first sight of the East, a 'whispered promise of mysterious delight' which for Marlow as much as for the young boys in the earlier stories carries inward, maturational significance. But Conrad's imaginative concern, like Ransome's and Masefield's, is with the experience of youth for its own sake, and the arduous processes by which its unforgettable epiphanies are won. This is Conrad's account of Marlow on *his* first command, in *his* small boat at sea:

I did not know how good a man I was till then. I remember the drawn faces, the dejected figures of my two men, and I remember my youth and the feeling that will never come back any more— the feeling that I could last for ever, outlast the sea, the earth, and all men; the deceitful feeling that lures us on to joys, to perils, to love, to vain effort--to death; the triumphant conviction of

130

strength, the heat of life in the handful of dust, the glow in the heart that with every year grows dim . . .

As Conrad wrote in the first sentence of *The Shadow-Line*: 'Only the young have such moments.' But in that great novel he subdivided life still further. The moments he referred to are 'of boredom, of weariness, of dissatisfaction'. They come when 'the little gate of mere boyishness' has closed, and when 'one perceives ahead a shadow-line warning one that the region of early youth, too, must be left behind.' *The Shadow-Line* is another story of first command, and it traces the process of maturity to its limit, when the conclusive ordeal of self-proof is generated by the 'green sickness of late youth' and comes to a man well into his twenties. It is one long, extended process, common to all people, boys and girls alike, and marked by a succession of great experiences. Those I have chosen in the texts considered here are only examples. We cannot all be captains. Perhaps not all of us can learn to swim. The key experiences are not the same for any two individuals, are not the same for boys and girls, or not necessarily so. Nor is the duration of 'youth', and the boundary of 'late youth' the same for two individuals or for both sexes. There is infinite diversity.

It does seem to me, however, that a concept of youth is necessary, and that a literature of youth (including film and television fictions) is necessary to articulate and support it. It seems to me also that such experiences as I have exemplified in this chapter (phrased in the title of one of Robert Westall's last novels as 'falling into glory') are necessary to effective growth, and that literature and story have an indispensable role to play in providing children with such images and mirrors of their private experiences and needs.

In social life, and in critiques of fiction, we can be so preoccupied with ideological appraisal of the institutions and stories providing these experiences that we forget the importance of the experience itself. Of course it matters what gives rise to such occasions, but it matters a great deal more if nothing does.

References & Other Books Discussed

Bracketed numbers before a title refer to the page in *Signs of Childness* on which the book is quoted.

[50] Joan Aiken, 'A Free Gift', *The Thorny Paradise: Writers on Writing for Children* (1975), ed. Edward Blishen, Kestrel Books, page 37

[87] Joan Aiken, *The Way to Write for Children* (1982), Elm Tree Books, page 72

[15] Brian Alderson, 'The Irrelevance of Children to the Children's Book Reviewer', *Children's Book News*, January/February 1969. Quoted in *Children's Literature: The Development of Criticism* (1990), ed. Peter Hunt, Routledge, pages 54-5

[74] Nina Bawden, 'A Dead Pig and My Father', *Children's Literature in Education* 14, May 1974. Reprinted in *Writers, Critics and Children* (1976), ed. Geoff Fox et al., Heinemann Educational Books, page 4

[41] Joseph Conrad, *Heart of Darkness*, in *Youth: A Narrative and Two Other Stories* (1902); many editions

[61, 131] Joseph Conrad, *The Shadow-Line* (1917), Dent; Collected Edition, *The Shadow-Line and Within the Tides*, 1950, page 3

[130-1] Joseph Conrad, 'Youth', in *Youth: A Narrative and Two Other Stories* (1902); many editions

[58-9] Hugh Cunningham, *Children and Childhood in Western Society since 1500* (1995), Longman, page 190

[110] Berlie Doherty, *White Peak Farm* (1984), Methuen, page 71

[71] Paul John Eakin, *Touching the World: Reference in Autobiography* (1992), Princeton University Press, pages 66-7

[103, 104-5] Leon Garfield, *Smith* (1967), Constable Young Books; Puffin Classics edition, 1994, pages 6, 77-8

[74] Alan Garner: 'An Interview with Alan Garner' by Aidan Chambers, *The Signal Approach to Children's Books* (1980), ed. Nancy Chambers, Kestrel Books, page 279

[57, 61] Christina Hardyment, 'Looking at Children: The History of Childhood 1600 to the Present', in Sara Holdsworth & Joan Crossley, *Innocence and Experience. Images of Children in British Art from 1600 to the Present*, Catalogue of the Exhibition originated by Manchester City Art Galleries and toured by the South Bank Centre, September 1992-April 1993, Manchester City Art Galleries, 1992, pages 93-4

[88] Susan Hill, *I'm the King of the Castle*, Longmans Imprint edition, 1981. Reprinted in Susan Hill, *The Lighting of the Lamps* (1987), Hamish Hamilton, page 60

[24] Peter Hunt, *Criticism, Theory and Children's Literature* (1991), Basil Blackwell, pages 61, 62

[30] Peter Hunt, a summary from *Criticism, Theory and Children's Literature* (1991), Basil Blackwell, pages 46-8

[50] Peter Hunt, as above, page 59

[50] R.D.S. Jack, *The Road to the Never Land: A Reassessment of J.M. Barrie's Dramatic Art* (1991), Aberdeen University Press, pages 165-6

[9] Henry James, 'The Future of the Novel' (1899). Reprinted in Henry James, *Selected Literary Criticism* (1981), ed. Morris Shapira, Cambridge University Press, page 181

[107] D.H. Lawrence, *The Rainbow* (1915), Heinemann; Phoenix edition, 1955, pages 220-1

Ursula Le Guin, *The Left Hand of Darkness* (1969), Macdonald

[42] Ursula Le Guin, 'This Fear of Dragons', *The Thorny Paradise* (1975), ed. Edward Blishen, Kestrel Books, pages 91-2

[51] Madeleine L'Engle, a paper given at the annual conference of the Louisiana Library Association (1964), reprinted in *A Sense of Story* (1971), ed. John Rowe Townsend, Longman, page 128

[123] Doris Lessing, 'Through the Tunnel', reprinted in *Short Stories of Our Time* (1963), ed. D.R. Barnes, Harrap, pages 91, 93

[26] C.S. Lewis, 'On Three Ways of Writing for Children', reprinted in *Only Connect: Readings on Children's Literature* (2nd edition, 1980), ed. Sheila Egoff et al., Oxford University Press, Toronto, page 208

[36, 37] Myles McDowell, 'Fiction for Children and Adults: Some Essential Differences', *Children's Literature in Education* 10, March 1973. Reprinted in *Writers, Critics and Children*, ed. Geoff Fox et al., quoted by Peter Hunt in *Criticism, Theory and Children's Literature* (1991), Basil Blackwell, page 63

[31] Ian McEwan, article on, *The Times—Saturday Review*, 27 June 1992

[130] John Masefield, *The Bird of Dawning* (1933), Heinemann; Penguin edition, 1964, page 105

[23-4] D.C. Muecke, *The Compass of Irony* (1969), Methuen, pages 7, 14

[83] Lissa Paul, 'Escape Claws: Cover Stories on *Lolly Willowes* and *Crusoe's Daughter*', *Signal* 63, September 1990, page 208

[126-7] Gary Paulsen, *The Voyage of the 'Frog'* (1991), Macmillan; Pan Piper, 1992, pages 76, 93

[122-3] Philippa Pearce, 'Return to Air', *What the Neighbours Did and Other Stories* (1972), Longman; Puffin Books, 1975, page 123

[90-1] Philippa Pearce, 'Time Present', *Travellers in Time* (1990), CLNE/Green Bay Publications, page 73

Philippa Pearce, *Tom's Midnight Garden* (1958), Oxford University Press

[50] Alexander Pope, quoted in A. Charles Babenroth, *English Childhood: Wordsworth's Treatment of Childhood in the Light of English Poetry from Prior to Crabbe* (1922), Columbia University Press, page 19

Beatrix Potter, *The Tale of Mr Tod* (1912), Warne

[39] J.B. Priestley, quoted in Malcolm Bradbury, *No, Not Bloomsbury* (1987), Deutsch, page 319

Philip Pullman, *The Shadow in the Plate* (1986), Oxford University Press

[26] Arthur Ransome, 'A Letter to the Editor', *Junior Book-shelf* 1.4 (1937). Quoted in Peter Hunt, *Children's Literature: The Development of Criticism* (1990), Routledge, page 34

[128] Arthur Ransome, *We Didn't Mean to Go to Sea* (1937), Cape; Puffin Books, 1969, page 187

[42-3] C. John Sommerville, *The Discovery of Childhood in Puritan England* (1992), University of Georgia Press, Athens, Georgia, page 10

[52] Sommerville, as above, pages 8-9

[60] Sommerville, as above, page 15

[74] Ivan Southall, from an article in *Horn Book*, June 1968. Reprinted in *A Sense of Story* (1971), ed. John Rowe Townsend, Longman, page 191

Catherine Storr, *Robin* (1962), Faber & Faber

[62-3] Catherine Storr, 'Why Write? Why Write for Children?' , *The Thorny Paradise* (1975), ed. Edward Blishen, Kestrel Books, page 27

[58] *The Sunday Times*, Charles Hymas, education correspondent, 28 February 1993

[75] Rosemary Sutcliff, 'Still in the Making', *School Bookshop News*, March 1976

[124] Graham Swift, 'Learning to Swim', *Learning to Swim and Other Stories* (1982), London Magazine Editions; Picador, 1985, page 146

[52] Keith Thomas, 'Children in Early Modern England', in *Children and Their Books: A Celebration of the Work of Iona and Peter Opie* (1989), eds. Gillian Avery & Julia Briggs, Clarendon Press, page 46

[26] John Rowe Townsend, 'Peering into the Fog: The Future of Children's Books', *Horn Book*, June 1977, page 348

[27] John Rowe Townsend, *A Sense of Story* (1971), Longman, page 10

[119] Geoffrey Trease, interview in *Rear Window* series, Channel 4, 26 May 1992

[125-6] Jill Paton Walsh, *Dolphin Crossing* (1967), Macmillan; Puffin Books, 1970, page 103

[40-1] Jill Paton Walsh, 'The Rainbow Surface', *Times Liter-*

ary Supplement, 3 December 1971. Reprinted in *Suitable for Children?* (1976) ed. Nicholas Tucker, Sussex University Press, pages 212-13

[64-5] Jill Paton Walsh, 'Seeing Green', *The Thorny Paradise* (1975), ed. Edward Blishen, Kestrel Books, page 59

[44] William Walsh, *The Use of Imagination* (1959), Chatto & Windus, page 137

[66, 68, 72] Mary Warnock, *Memory* (1987), Faber & Faber, pages 145, 135

[32, 33-5] Mary Warnock, 'Escape into Childhood', *New Society*, 1971, Volume 17, page 823

Sylvia Waugh, *Mennyms Under Siege (*1995), Julia MacRae Books

[117, 118] H.G. Wells, 'The Door in the Wall', in *The Short Stories of H.G. Wells* (1927), Benn, pages 167-8, 170, 178

[112] Robert Westall, *The Machine-Gunners* (1975), Macmillan; Puffin Books, 1977, pages 94, 135

[114, 115] Robert Westall, *Yaxley's Cat* (1991), Macmillan; Pan Piper, 1992, pages 64, 125-6, 129

Index